A HEART ABLAZE

IGNITING A PASSION FOR GOD

MISSION GUIDE

JOHN BEVERE

Requests for information should be addressed to:
Messenger International
P. O. Box 888, Palmer Lake, CO 80133-0888
www.messengerintl.org

Project Management and Media Consultant
www.vaughnstreet.com

COVER AND INTERIOR DESIGN:
Eastco Multi Media Solutions, Inc
3646 California Rd.
Orchard Park, NY 14127
www.eastcomultimedia.com

Writer: Holt Vaughn
Editor: Deborah Moss
Design Manager: Jon La Porta
Designers: Jon La Porta, Aaron La Porta, Heather Wierowski

Printed in the United States of America

TABLE OF CONTENTS

I'd like to welcome you to *A Heart Ablaze: Igniting a Passion for God.* This is a very timely and extremely powerful message! It is so needed in the church and the world today as we seek to be a people whose hearts show forth the glory of Almighty God in our obedience to Him. I believe it will transform your life and family and impact your church in ways you may never have dreamed or imagined. You will see eternal fruit from what this message produces in your life with the Lord.

God has blessed our outreach beyond what I had imagined as I've seen our other curricula touch hundreds of thousands of people in thousands of churches throughout the world.

This curriculum will take you on a mission to a place where you can actually live the reality of a transformed life-a life of passion, glory, and holy power! Intimacy with the Holy Spirit, obedience to God, and a fruitful life full of fiery glory are available to each of us! More than just knowing about God and what He does, you can actually know God and who He is! You will be transformed by the renewing of your heart and mind, and you can carry His grace and glory to multitudes of others.

I want you to know that we are not going to be following a set of rules or some dry type of legalism. *A Heart Ablaze* is actually a mission of transformation, not by fleshly works but by the Holy Spirit's empowerment through the grace given to every believer. It is a lifelong passion you can have as you experience the fire of God Himself!

Let's join together and begin right now to set our hearts afire! You will find the Word of God, the life of the Father and the presence of the Holy Spirit to be the most energizing, exhilarating, and transforming experience you have ever known!

EASY-TO-USE INSTRUCTIONS
for Students

Easy-to-Use Student Instructions...

- Start your mission by reading the book *A Heart Ablaze, Igniting A Passion For God*. Don't be afraid to underline or write in the book. Be prayerful, and keep your Bible handy as you read. As you go, remember to make notes and mark pages for any questions you may have.
- There are twelve video sessions, each of which corresponds to a chapter in the Workbook.
- The answers to the questions are taken from the book and the videos.
- A complete transcript of each video session is available by contacting Messenger International at US (toll Free) 1-800-648-1477, Australia 1-300-650-577, or UK 44 (0) 870-745-5790

GROUP STUDY...

- Before each group session, find out how your group leader wants to organize the sessions. You may be asked to complete the video and workbook chapter before the session. Others may prefer that you wait until the group meets to do the workbook questions. Follow the instructions your group leader gives you, as this is only a guide.

- As you watch the video with the group, use the spaces provided for answers.

- Enjoy the video. You don't have to keep up with all the questions and answers.

- During each session, your group leader will provide answers and facilitate discussions. Whether you are a "people" person or more reserved, you will get much more out of this journey if you pray and ask the Holy Spirit to lead you as an active participant. Prayer is essential to your life's mission, so spend quality time with the Lord before you come to each session.

- There will be times for prayer and ministry throughout the sessions. Go to each session expectant that the Lord will move!

PERSONAL STUDY...

- If you have purchased this curriculum and are not part of a group, simply watch each video session with your workbook open. You can watch one time through and take notes, and then go back and fill in all the answers while referring to the video, or you can pause the video and fill in the answers as you go.

JOURNALING

One of the features of this mission is that it includes times of "journaling" or recording thoughts, prayers and feelings in many of the sessions. This may be new to you. Webster's dictionary defines journaling as "a record of experiences, ideas, or reflections kept regularly for private use." In the Old Testament, God told His people to write things down, so they could be passed down from generation to generation. Of course, we have the New Testament for the simple reason that it was written down as a record of the words and works of Jesus and His disciples. We are to keep His words written upon our hearts, and journaling is an excellent way to accomplish this.

The following are not all hard and fast rules, but they are helpful suggestions for the journaling portions of this mission:

- Always record the date and time.
- Follow the instructions for each particular journaling portion. Record feelings: good, bad, or indifferent.
- Make note of thoughts and images that the Holy Spirit brings before you and write down Bible verses that come alive to you.
- Write what God tells and reveals to you, even if you do not fully understand it.

You'll quickly find that as God sets your heart ablaze, He will start speaking to you more than ever before! Therefore, you may want to start a journal of your own if you don't already have one to use in addition to the spaces provided in the workbook.

Journaling can be an invaluable tool for years to come. Journaling will help you understand how God is working in your life as you see your progress and gain clarity in your walk with God. You will be able to look back and see the amazing works God has accomplished in your life as you've grown in intimacy with Him. It will be a great source of inspiration and faith to keep your heart on fire for God. It will be a way to enable you to share with others the wonderful testimony of what God has done in your life.

A HEART ABLAZE, IGNITING A PASSION FOR GOD

Mission One

Psalm 104:4 says, *"[God] makes…His ministers a flame of fire."*

MISSION: POSSIBLE

1.) Welcome. You are starting something miraculous. Rather than simply gathering more information, you will experience *transformation.* You are going to permanently turn up the heat of your relationship with the Father God, Jesus, and the Holy Spirit! **This is no ordinary study; this is your *personal mission* to experience the glory of a changed life…the power and peace of a holy life with God…a relationship that positively, permanently transforms you and deeply touches others.**

A mission is a special assignment or objective. What is the Scripture verse that is the mission of this course?

Phil 2:15   Dan 12-3   Ps 104-4   Luke 3-7

2.) Your Personal Mission Statement

Sports, business, academics, religion, the arts, and politics—it's a fact that the world's highest achievers in any field typically have their own "personal mission statement."

Here is a guideline of what a personal mission statement looks like:
1. It is a short written statement that is easy to remember.
2. It is posted where you can see it regularly.
- 3. It will have specific goals.
4. And it will have a timeline for making that goal.

Now here is a simple but excellent example for you to learn from. Read it several times. **Notice that it is *short* and contains *specific goals, tasks,* and a *timeline*:**

~My goal is to help my company grow 20 percent this year and to increase my salary. To accomplish this I will complete my MBA degree within twelve months by devoting eight hours per week to my Internet college degree program. I will daily apply what I learn, increasing my value to the company and qualifying for promotion.~

While this example deals with a person's career goals, there are personal *spiritual* mission statements, too.

Take the time to write your own personal mission statement for *A Heart Ablaze.* Remember to <u>follow the guidelines above</u>. This is a defining moment for you as you take responsibility for your walk with God. Seek God's heart on this as you write. You may want to review it and perfect it at the end of this first session:

MY PERSONAL MISSION STATEMENT FOR *A HEART ABLAZE*:

✓   *Hunger for God*

3.) Mission Prayer: Lord, I come to You in the mighty name of Jesus. I want to be Your minister—a flame of fire. Help me by Your Holy Spirit to follow through and fulfill this mission. I trust You, Lord, and I rely upon You to shape me, form me, mold me, instruct me, break me, build me, rebuke me, comfort me, and complete in me the purposes You have for me as I go through this *A Heart Ablaze* course. I look strongly to You, Father God, to create in me a clean heart, a heart ablaze with the fire of Your vision, Your will, and Your mission for me on this earth. *I am not alone in this; I will complete this mission by Your power.* Amen!

Signed: _____ (Sign your name here)

Date: _____

4.) Jesus said, *"You are the light of the world"* (Matt. 5:14), and John the Baptist said that Jesus would *"baptize you with the Holy Spirit and fire"* (Luke 3:16).

If you begin to shine with God's light, you will __overcome__ the atmosphere you're in.

5.)  **History Makers**

Throughout history God has used people from all walks of life to shape, change, and make history. YOU CAN BE A HISTORY MAKER, TOO! Whether you are a leader of nations or an "average" person, God can use you to shape events, help your neighbor, transform lives, and daily impact the world.

Scripture teaches that we can learn from history as we observe the "great cloud of witnesses" that have gone before us.

> *"Now all these things happened to them as examples, and they were written for our admonition, upon whom the ends of the ages have come."*
> —1 Corinthians 10:11

> *"Therefore we also, since we are surrounded by so great a cloud of witnesses, let us lay aside every weight, and the sin which so easily ensnares us, and let us run with endurance the race that is set before us."*
> —Hebrews 12:1

In the Welsh revival that shook an entire nation in the late 1800s, the person who sparked the flame igniting the church was a young man named **Evan Roberts.** He simply gave himself to the Lord as he served in the church, studied the Bible and the great theological books of his day, and boldly began praying fervently. For more than ten years he did these things faithfully. Alone and with others, Evan sought God continually and regularly, imploring the Lord to mold and bend him and send revival to his nation. Society and culture itself were transformed as God responded mightily. The crime rate dropped, drunkards were reformed, and foul language disappeared. Even football and rugby became uninteresting in the light of God's glory that was poured out. Young people would forsake sin, housewives would become flaming evangelists in their neighborhoods, and even the authorities in the established church and politics were set on fire for God's purposes.

Can you think of at least three biblical examples of men and women, young and old, who *changed* and *shaped history?*

1.

2.

3.

You can learn from each example you chose: What took place, how did it *happen?*

1.

2.

3.

6.) You've seen how God works in others. But how and what could **you** do to be a history maker in your life right now?

7.) *"O Corinthians! We have spoken openly to you, our heart is wide open. You are not restricted by us, but you are restricted by your own affections."* —2 Corinthians 6:11–12

Our own _lust & affections_ are what restrict us. There is freedom in _Submission_ to God, and there is _bondage_ when you feel like you are walking free from God's authority. True freedom can only be found in submission to _Gods_ authority. True freedom can only be found in _submission_ to what God desires.

8.) God is seeking to dwell in us, and we are to come out from among the world so He may receive us as we set ourselves apart to be holy.

James 4:4 in the New Living Translation says, *"If your aim is to enjoy this world, you can't be a friend of God."*

The New International Version gets a little bit stronger, saying, *"Anyone who chooses to be a friend of the world becomes an enemy of God."*

Is James writing this to Christians or unbelievers? Christians

How do you know? 15 time my Brethren

God's promises are not automatic
They are conditional. He is seeking a dwelling place that honors Him.

9.) The Message Bible puts it this way in 2 Corinthians 6:17: *"'So leave the corruption and compromise; leave it for good,' says God. 'Don't link up with those who will pollute you. I want you all for myself.'"*

What does this mean to you in terms of practical application? How can you apply this truth to your life, starting today, as you forsake the corruption and compromise of the world? Remember your personal mission statement as you answer this important question.

10.) *"And what agreement hath the temple of God with idols? For ye are the temple of the living God; as God hath said, I will dwell in them, and walk in them; and I will be their God, and they shall be my people. Wherefore come out from among them, and be ye separate, saith the Lord, and touch not the unclean thing; and I will receive you, And will be a Father unto you, and ye shall be my sons and daughters, saith the Lord Almighty. Having therefore these promises, dearly beloved, let us cleanse ourselves from all filthiness of the flesh and spirit, perfecting holiness in the fear of God."* —2 Corinthians 6:16–18; 7:1, KJV

What are the four promises given in this passage?

1. dwell w/ you

2. Walk among you

3. be you God

4. you'll be my people

A Bush Ablaze

11 a.) True/False: Moses' destination when he delivers Israel from the captivity of Egypt is to go into the Promised Land.

11 b.) True/False: Moses' destination when he delivers Israel from the captivity of Egypt is to take them to the wilderness to worship God.

12 a.) What would have resulted if Moses had brought Israel out of Egypt straight into the Promised Land without first bringing them to the Promiser (God)?

idolatry

12 b.) Why does God bring Moses to the back side of the desert (and later Israel to the wilderness)?

— To quite His self —

12 c.) Often God leads us into circumstances that seem difficult, uncomfortable, or downright impossible. Yet in these desert places we can know God in ways we never would have otherwise! What wilderness-type experiences have you come through? Think about it: *The lessons you learned from these are precious!* They can help you embrace God's purposes in the future instead of rejecting His leadings and His very presence! Record here some of your very own personal lessons to live by next time you are faced with the wilderness:

13 a.) What is the whole object of our being set free? To come into the

The knowledge of of God.

13 b.) In John 17:3, what did Jesus say was eternal life?

"And this is eternal life, that they may _know_, the only true God, and Jesus Christ whom You have sent."

14.) Leadership that has the _incorrect focus_ is worse than no leadership at all.

Your mission, your highest purpose

15.) *"You have seen what I did to the Egyptians, and how I bore you on eagles' wings and brought you to Myself."* —Exodus 19:4

True/False: You can rejoice and fulfill your mission because God created you and saved you for one purpose: To bring you to Himself.

"And do not be conformed to this world, but be transformed by the renewing of your mind, that you may prove what is that good and acceptable and perfect will of God."
—Romans 12:2

The children of Israel felt they knew their destination when they left Egypt, but God's purposes and plans were very different from their imaginations. They thought they were going to *a place* to *get blessed*, but God wanted to bring them to a person: **HIMSELF!**

Review your personal mission statement. Have you written what you think or what God *desires?* As we continue, we will be looking at the difference between those two ideals. Be open to *God*—where He is leading you is to HIMSELF! As you are transformed by the renewing of your mind, you may see the need to constantly "tweak" your original statement. Use this book to grow. Write in it, make notes, journal, and scribble your thoughts in it—that's what it's for as the Lord leads you to Himself!

A HEART ABLAZE, IGNITING A PASSION FOR GOD

Mission Two

James 2:19 says, *"You believe that there is one God. You do well. Even the demons believe—and tremble!"*

MISSION: IT'S NOT JUST ABOUT BELIEVING, IT'S ABOUT OBEYING.

1.) You saw in the first session that God delivered His people out of the cruel bondage of Egypt to bring them to Himself (Exod. 19:4). This is a type of our salvation and deliverance from the world. The Lord calls us out of darkness, out of spiritual and worldly bondage, and brings us into His light, His freedom, and His Kingdom.

 In at least one application, *A Heart Ablaze* could be summed up as God saying, "I have delivered you out of Egypt (the world and its ungodly ways); now get Egypt out of you!"

"Coming to Him as to a living stone, rejected indeed by men, but chosen by God and precious, you also, as living stones, are being built up a spiritual house, a holy priest-hood, to offer up spiritual sacrifices acceptable to God through Jesus Christ. Therefore it is also contained in the Scripture, 'Behold, I lay in Zion a chief cornerstone, elect, precious, and he who believes on Him will by no means be put to shame.' Therefore, to you who believe, He is precious; but to those who are disobedient, 'The stone which the builders rejected has become the chief cornerstone,' and 'a stone of stumbling and a rock of offense.' They stumble, being disobedient to the word, to which they also were appointed. But you are a chosen generation, a royal priesthood, a holy nation, His own special people, that you may proclaim the praises of Him who called you out of darkness into His marvelous light." —I Peter 2:4–9

Review your personal mission statement from the first session. Make any changes necessary to improve upon it. Then pray again—not only the Mission Prayer from session one, but also add your own thoughts and prayers to it as God deals with you and blesses you in your time with Him. Be open to His leading, correction, and instruction as you continue on this course. Write here any significant things the Lord has shared with you so far:

_____

_____

_____

_____

_____

_____

_____

Date: _____

2.) There are vital and rich truths that come forth within the very first minutes of this video session. Complete the following sentences:

a.   If you believe in Jesus, you'll _____ Jesus.

b.   The evidence of your belief is your _____.

c.   In many of today's churches we have been led into the error of simply getting

        people to acknowledge that Jesus _____.

d.   True/False: Demons have more fear of God than some people in the church.

e.   True/False: Jesus is called the rock of offense and a stumbling stone.

f.   His Word will be offensive at times. Why? It will _____

        the way in you that is _____ to a Holy God.

g.   This is why we as believers are to _____ being corrected.

h.   True believers have been made a royal priesthood. Why? Because only

_____ can minister to royalty. Only royalty can come

into _____ of royalty and speak in intimate terms.

i.   _____ can come to a certain level, but when you want to
      have intimate fellowship, only royalty can minister to royalty and have fellowship
      with royalty.

3.) The gospel is not a dry and dead religion. It is a well of living water within us that
transforms our very lives and then springs forth to impact the lives of others. Obedience
to the gospel isn't about a set of rules, regulations, and laws, but rather it is a loving
response in the relationship we have with our Lord. Look at 2 Corinthians 6:17 in the
King James Version:

 *"Wherefore come out from among them, and be ye separate, saith the Lord, and touch
not the unclean thing; and I will receive you."*

Some get the impression that this means we are not supposed to associate in any way
with unbelievers. Yet Mark 16:15 clearly states *"And he said unto them, Go ye into all the
world, and preach the gospel to every creature"* (KJV). How do you apply both of these
scriptures to your life?

REACHING OUT

4.) *"Thus, by their fruit you will recognize them. Not everyone who says to me, 'Lord, Lord,' will enter the kingdom of heaven, but only he who does the will of my Father who is in heaven."* —Matthew 7:20–21, NIV

Two things to watch for on your mission.
You will experience at least two ways that the Holy Spirit ministers to you in these sessions.

One of these is the way He will transform you on the *inside*, in *your* heart. We'll call this **Transformed Within**, and you will see this frequently in this workbook as you fulfill your mission.

"For it is God who works in you both to will and to do for His good pleasure."
—Philippians 2:13

The second is how He will lead you to *reach out* to others as you live out your inner faith with the good works and fruit of your obedience. Reaching out is the fruit of your intimate relationship with God! You will see this frequently in your workbook as well.

Here are some suggested ways in which anyone can live out their faith, reaching out to others:

~   Pray with a prayer partner about an unsaved family member and then invite that family member to church with you.
~   Pray, then invite a co-worker to lunch and develop a relationship of witnessing to him or her.
~   Pray, then give someone who needs the Lord a Christian CD or a book or magazine about a subject they would be interested in; for example, a book about golf, sports, music, or business. All of these are easy and effective ways to reach out with the life you have within!

Write the NAMES of two needy people you could reach out to:

1.

2.

Now write HOW you could reach out to them (invite to church, give a book, take to lunch, etc):

1.
2.

If you are doing the *Ablaze* course with a group, consider giving someone an invitation to come to the group *Ablaze* meetings that you are a part of. Or if you are doing it individually, tell people about it when they ask you, "How's it going?" or "What's up?" What a great opportunity to simply answer their question about your life and open the door to give them GOD'S LIFE!

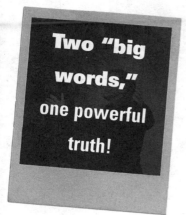
5.) If doing these great works is not the focus of Christianity, what is the focus?

6.) God didn't save you so He could use you. He saved you because He desired to

_____ intimately and for you to _____

intimately. That is the _____ you were created.

Two "big words," one powerful truth!

7.) God said to Moses, *"Go to the people and consecrate them"* (Exod. 19:10). What does the word consecrate mean? It means to

_____. And what does sanctify mean?

_____

8.) "Consecrate" and "sanctify" are not negative or legalistic words or ideas. How does the story of Esther illustrate this?

9.) What parallels with Esther can you see in your own salvation experience? How has God taken you from where you were in your life in the past, blessed and ministered to you, and given you new life?

10.) Currently, up to this point in your life, what are some of the specific ways by which you have *already* set yourself apart for God?

11.) Second Corinthians 7:1 says, *"Therefore, having these promises..."* What promises? Of God dwelling in us, walking among us, and of Him being our God and us being His people. It goes on to say, *"Let us cleanse ourselves from all filthiness of the flesh and spirit."*

So you see here that you have a responsibility. You have the Holy Spirit in you, and you must cleanse yourself from the filth of the garment of the flesh and the garment of the spirit.

Why did Moses tell the people of Israel who came out of Egypt to wash their clothes?

Because they still had _____ on them from Egypt.

What is God saying to you here? He is saying that it's _____

responsibility to cleanse yourself. You've been delivered out of the world, and now

_____ have to get the world out of yourself.

Prepare for His coming!

12.) What are some ways you can *further* cleanse yourself, consecrating your life to the Lord? Write some specific ways you can set yourself apart for God right now and in the future in your life.

13.) *"Grace and peace be multiplied to you in the knowledge of God and of Jesus our Lord, as His divine power has given to us all things that pertain to life and godliness, through the knowledge of Him who called us by glory and virtue, by which have been given to us exceedingly great and precious promises, that through these you may be partakers of the divine nature, having escaped the corruption that is in the world through lust."*

—2 Peter 1:2–4

If you preach that we are just _____ saved by grace and we're no _____ from the sinners, then that's the kind of _____, and _____ church you're going to have.

But when you preach to the church that we are the _____ of God and you have been _____ to _____ yourself from filthiness, you're going to have power.

14.) What is the confusion between justification and sanctification, and how can you work it out?

15.) Jesus supplies _____ for our sanctification, but we must _____ by _____ ourselves through the power of that grace.

"Jesus is coming for His church, a pure bride, whether people are ready or not. He's coming in His glory, and it would be good for you to be sanctified and ready for His coming. The people of Israel really believed they were ready, but they were not."

- John Bevere

Are you Ready?

A HEART ABLAZE, IGNITING A PASSION FOR GOD

Mission Three

Isaiah 60:1 says, *"Arise, shine; for your light has come!
And the glory of the LORD is risen upon you."*

MISSION: NEVER LOSE SIGHT OF THE AWE-INSPIRING GLORY OF GOD

1.) A drama is building in this series as we move from session to session in the videos and from chapter to chapter in the *A Heart Ablaze* book. Our mission is to gain an understanding of and be transformed by some very necessary and profound truths that at times have been lost among us.

One of these is the magnitude of what God has promised us. Another is to understand—get a grasp on—the awe-inspiring glory and majesty of our Lord!

Refresh your memory and your heart. This brief review will help spark the flame:
- God has given us great and precious promises.
- He has brought us to Himself that He may dwell among us.
- His passion is to dwell in us, intimately walking with us.
- This is the very purpose behind His bringing Israel out of the bondage of Egypt and for bringing you out of the bondage of Satan and the world.
- We are to cooperate with the Holy Spirit, cleansing ourselves from the impurities of the flesh and the world, setting ourselves apart for the glory of the Lord, preparing for His coming.

Now, *in your own words* write down some of the truths that, *applied to your own life*, have burned within your own heart up to this point in this series. What have you learned, and what do you feel God may be speaking to you?

2.) When God came in His glory as described in Hebrews 12:21 and Exodus 19, there was the loud blaring of a trumpet blast, constant roaring thundering, lightning flashes, massive fire and smoke, and a violent quaking of the earth. The people of Israel shook with fright; even Moses was terrified and trembling!

Hebrews 13:8 says God is the same yesterday today and forever. Could it be that there is more to God's glory than we have understood? What can you learn from these passages in Hebrews and Exodus?

3.) How does this biblical description of God's glory compare with your current perceptions of God's glory?

4.) Do you believe that reverence and fear are part of the experience of God's glory? Why?

5.) "Our diminished estimation of God's nature is an evil of great magnitude. It effaces our conception of sin and destroys our sensitivity to right and wrong. We begin to think that God is indifferent to the distinctions between sin and holiness" —E.M. Bounds[1]

The very nature of God and the glory of God are intertwined. God IS holiness, He IS justice, He IS purity, and so much more. *You may have never before come across this truth that we can* become too familiar, too confident in the presence of God. *What is your initial reaction to the concept?*

6.) Do you have a low estimation of God's glory? Do you take Him for granted? Make this question even more personal: What are some ways that *you* may have become too familiar, too confident in the presence of God?

7.) Now that you've faced it, how can you change that?

8.) **Fear of the Lord is part of God's glory**

And I say to you, My friends, do not be afraid of those who kill the body, and after that have no more that they can do. But I will show you whom you should fear: Fear Him who, after He has killed, has power to cast into hell; yes, I say to you, fear Him!
—Luke 12:4–5

Some say, "The truth hurts." But God's truth comes with a healing balm. The fact is God is not a man. He is God. There is an infinite difference between Him and His creation. Thankfully God Himself bridged that gap through Christ, so the fear of hell can be removed. Yet He is still God and we are His creation, loved and blessed as we serve Him, but nonetheless we are but dust that He has breathed His life into. Everything we are and have is a gift from Him. Every breath we take is by His grace. To behold the true God is too much to fathom.

E. M. Bounds (1835–1913) was one of the great teachers and preachers of the 1800s on the subject of prayer and revival. He saw the raw stuff of life as a young gold miner, then at twenty-one years of age as a practicing attorney. He later became a pastor, teacher, writer, and church leader. Bounds was also a Civil War chaplain who lived firsthand the ravages of war. In some of the toughest battles, having himself

been imprisoned and wounded, he experienced some of the worst of human fears. He came to understand the fear and glory of his God as well. Today his seasoned words are revered among thousands worldwide. Let's look at some of his insights:

"Fear of the right kind is a mighty force…The New Testament deals largely in the element of fear, and in a more radical, powerful and startling way than the Old Testament…The early disciples are represented as 'walking in the fear of the Lord.' New Testament holiness is to be perfected in 'the fear of the Lord.' We are charged to cover our whole Christian career with this principle and to 'pass the time of our sojourning in fear' and to serve with 'godly fear.' In heaven they utter the cry of amazement 'Who shall not fear thee, O Lord.' And there issues from the throne the decree that that is to sway heaven and earth: 'Praise our God, all ye his servants, and ye that fear him.' These quotations are enough to show that the New Testament neither discards, nor discredits the motive of fear as an element in the purist and strongest piety." —E.M. Bounds[2]

Is this subject new to you? Did you ever realize there was the fear of the Lord in both the Old and New Testaments? What is God speaking to you as you read the quote from E. M. Bounds about the role of godly fear in the life of the believer?

9.) In what ways do you think fear (both spiritually and naturally) can be a positive force or motivator?

10.) ## The **Wonder** of God

"Lord, how great is our dilemma! In Thy Presence silence becomes us, but love inflames our hearts and constrains us to speak." —A. W. Tozer[3]

"That God can be known by the soul in tender personal experience while remaining infinitely aloof from the curious eyes of reason constitutes a paradox best described as darkness to the intellect but sunshine to the heart."

—Frederick W. Faber
—A.W. Tozer[4]

"I have uttered what I did not understand, Things too wonderful for me, which I did not know. Listen, please, and let me speak; You said, 'I will question you, and you shall answer Me.' I have heard of You by the hearing of the ear, but now my eye sees You. Therefore I abhor myself, and repent in dust and ashes." —Job 42:3–6

The God of the galaxies, of all creation, has called us to Himself! While it is so very true and important for us to acknowledge that God's glory is incomprehensible, unapproachable, and completely divine, He has given us glimpses of His greatness. We simply behold His creation, His wonders.

- The universe contains billions of galaxies.
- Each of those billions of galaxies contains billions of individual stars.
- A light year is how far light travels in one year. Light travels at 186,282 miles *per second, 670,000,000 miles per hour.*
- Our sun is 93,000,000 miles away. If you were to leave on a nonstop commercial jet flight to the sun, it would take 21 *years.* By car would take *200 years* provided you didn't stop at any restaurants or hotels.
- The closest star to earth is 4.3 light years away. In a scale model, our sun could appear as a soccer ball, the earth as a peppercorn would be 26 yards away, and the closest star would appear 4000 miles away!

Scale size of Soccer Ball = "Our Sun"
Scale size of Peppercorn = "Earth"

Boston, MA

4000 Miles Away

Peppercorn
(only 26 yds. away)

Soccer Ball
in San Diego, CA

- When you walk outside at night, there are some stars you can see that are 4,000 *light years* away. The light you are seeing from that star left that star about the time Sarah married Abraham, has been traveling 670,000,000 miles per hour, and *is just now getting here!*
- Andromeda, a galaxy very close to ours, is 2.3 *million light years* away.
- There is a quadrant of the universe that a telescope found with galaxies that were 13,000,000,000 (13 BILLION) *light years* away
- **Yet God has said, "I measured one end to the other with the span of my hand."** (See Isaiah 40:12.)

Check as many as this inspires in you:
[ ] awe [ ] fear [ ] wonder [ ] doubt / skepticism [ ] the need to study more

[ ] the need to pray more [ ] faith [ ] worship [ ] intimidation [ ] interest

11.) Take some time to pray and meditate on these things, then use your own words to describe what you feel.

12.) What are some of life's other wonders that challenge or inspire you as to God's greatness?

13.) *"So I said: 'Woe is me, for I am undone! Because I am a man of unclean lips, and I dwell in the midst of a people of unclean lips; for my eyes have seen the King, the Lord of hosts.'"* —Isaiah 6:5

Isaiah was a godly man, a priest, and a great prophet, yet he had just one glimpse of the Lord and cried out, "Woe is me." Moses himself was terrified and trembling at the glory of God, as we saw in Hebrews 12:21. Why do even the "great" men and women of God fear the Lord?

14.) *"And He said to me, 'My grace is sufficient for you, for My strength is made perfect in weakness.'"* —2 Corinthians 12:9

A paradox is something that is seemingly contradictory but may nonetheless be true. Second Corinthians 12:9 fits that description well. How can strength be made perfect in weakness? Aren't they opposites? Yet in God it is a fundamental spiritual truth which we must learn and live.

Have you seen a paradox in this session of *A Heart Ablaze*? There is a correlation between the spiritual stature of the men and women who serve God and their level of awe, humility, and fear toward God. **It is a great truth and paradox of the universe: Those who walk in deepest intimacy with Christ and become the most blessed servants of God seem to be the very ones who fear God the most!** How can this be? How do fear and intimacy go hand in hand? Why is it so? What "miracle" takes place when we rightly perceive God's glory?

Through His Glory God causes us to glorify Him!

15 a.) *"O Lord, our Lord, how excellent is Your name in all the earth, who have set Your glory above the heavens!...When I consider Your heavens, the work of Your fingers, the moon and the stars, which You have ordained, what is man that You are mindful of him, and the son of man that You visit him?"* —Psalm 8:1, 3–4

Have you ever felt as David did in this psalm? Humbled by the fact that the God of the universe has graciously blessed you? David knew that the purpose of understanding the greatness and glory of God is NOT to feel worthless or useless or insignificant. **The very reason that God came in the Person of Jesus Christ was because God so values us! But the church must keep the Lord exalted in His proper place—He is Majesty, The King of Kings, Creator God, Alpha Omega, Author and Finisher, Judge of all, pure light. In Him is no darkness.**

"As David did"

Step out in boldness. Even if you may not feel abundantly blessed with creativity, ask the Lord's direction and blessing. Write a psalm, song, or some creative expression of your heart and meditations to the Lord—as David did when he was moved on by God about these very beautiful and intense truths.

15 b.) There are times when the Lord will manifest Himself with and without His glory. If a king who had millions of people in his kingdom were to walk down the streets of a city with a Polo shirt on and a pair of shorts, with no attendants, you might walk right past him and not even recognize him. Why? _____.

In the Old Testament:

In Genesis 18 God came, but not in His glory, and ate a meal with Abraham.

In Genesis 32 Jacob wrestled with God as with a man, but it was certainly not God in all His glory.

Remember Joshua, in Joshua 5:13. He saw the Lord and didn't even know who He was. He said, "Are you for us or for our adversaries?" God said, "Neither, I'm the commander of the Host of the Lord." Do you remember what happened then? Joshua took off his shoes and worshiped. It was _____; it was not an

_____. Joshua saw the Lord but didn't even recognize Him.

Why? _____

In the New Testament:

In John 20:14, who was the first person who saw Jesus after He was raised from the dead? _____ She thought He was the gardener.

In Luke 24 Jesus walked on the Road of Emmaus with two disciples. They didn't know who He was. It wasn't until He took the bread and broke it, and then vanished from their sight, that they realized it was Jesus. That was after His resurrection, but He wasn't in His glory.

In John 21 the apostle John had breakfast with Jesus by the Sea of Tiberias. Some of the disciples were out fishing, but they hadn't caught anything. Then Jesus said, "Throw the net on the other side and you will find some." So they threw it and caught some fish, and John declared, "It's the Lord." Peter jumps in and swims to the shore, the others come in, and Jesus has breakfast cooking for them. This was after He was raised from the dead. He appeared to them but _____.

In His glory

In Revelation 1:12–16, the same apostle John who had breakfast with Jesus by the sea also saw Him on the deserted island of Patmos, but he was in the spirit.

Notice the difference: *"Then I turned to see the voice that spoke with me. And having turned I saw seven golden lampstands and in the midst of the seven lampstands, one like the Son of Man, clothed with a garment down to the feet and girded about the chest with a golden band. His head and hair were white like wool, as white as snow. His eyes were like a flame of fire; His feet were like fine brass, as it was refined in a furnace, and His voice as the sound of many waters; He had in His right hand seven stars, out of His mouth went a sharp two-edged sword, and His countenance was like the sun shining in its strength."*

"I want to show you what the glory of God is because I'm telling you something, I hear people say all the time, 'Man, the glory fell in that meeting.' I don't think so, because you wouldn't be here to tell me about it!"
—John Bevere

We've seen God in two ways.

1. Clothed in His glory: On the mountain in fire, smoke, thundering voice, and quaking, violent, earth-shaking glory. In heaven white as snow, as a flame of fire, like the sun.

2. Clothed in His humanity: As a seemingly common man, crucified like a criminal, at times not even recognized by those closest to Him.

Can you imagine being the father of children and having to hide yourself? Only being able to talk to them behind a curtain and not being able to just walk out and hold them? God desires to wrap His arms around us, showing us His glory.

Give God the opportunity to TRANSFORM YOU. Take this truth to the Lord in prayer.

First, write here your initial reaction to this subject. What does it mean to you personally? How can you change your thinking, attitudes, and actions to see more of God's glory in your life and the lives of others? Sort out your feelings and thoughts, and record them here now. Then pray and write more later as the Lord shows YOU more of Himself and His glory!

Date:_____

Revelation 22:3–5 is our destiny as we set ourselves apart for God and live in His glory!

And there shall be no more curse, but the throne of God and of the Lamb shall be in it, and His servants shall serve Him. They shall see His face, and His name shall be on their foreheads. There shall be no night there: They need no lamp nor light of the sun, for the Lord God gives them light. And they shall reign forever and ever.

A HEART ABLAZE, IGNITING A PASSION FOR GOD

Mission Four

The apostle Paul says in Philippians 2:12, *"Therefore, my dear friends, as you have always obeyed—not only in my presence, but now much more in my absence—continue to work out your salvation with fear and trembling."*

MISSION: PERSONAL RESPONSIBILITY. WORK OUT YOUR OWN SALVATION WITH FEAR AND TREMBLING.

1.) You are a child of God, and God passionately desires you to be as His Son: free and strong in the knowledge of who you are and what you are called to do!

Now, let's not just review, but let's keep this as real as possible. God has gotten you out of Egypt; now you are to get Egypt out of you.

So what does that mean anyway? **What are some areas in your everyday life that, when looked at honestly, you can still see some—maybe even a lot—of "Egypt" in those areas?** Keep in mind that now is not the time to worry about your image. Nothing is a secret to God anyway, so consider this an encounter with Him to help you be transformed more into His image: free, strong, holy, and joyfully set apart for the great things of a life on fire for God.

Some examples of these **areas** in your life may be: work, church, school, relationships with family, your thought life, your view of the opposite sex, or your choice of friends. *Be real, be specific, and let God do His work!*

2.)   How about **situations? What are some real-life** *situations* **you can see yourself in** (alone or with friends, family, work, school, etc.) **where your actions may look more like a captive slave of Pharaoh's Egypt than a free and empowered child of the King of the universe?**

Some examples may be: arguments with your spouse, handling your kids, confrontations at your job, your ability to say "no," your choices of entertainment and pleasure, what you read, what you watch and listen to, or how you react in a competitive environment. *What real-life situations are a continual challenge for you?*

3.)   God's glory is everything that makes God, God. It is the immeasurable weight and magnitude of God Himself. He is fire, thundering, and pure light. The apostle John saw Jesus in His glory and fell down as a dead man. And yet this same God has given you the grace and power to cleanse *yourself* in a divine and blessed cooperation with Himself. He never said He would do it all *for* you.

The Living Bible puts Philippians 2:13 this way: *"For God is at work within you, helping you want to obey him, and then helping you do what he wants."*

TRANSFORMED WITHIN

For it is God who works in you both to will and to do for His good pleasure.
Philippians 2:13

YOU HAVE A HUGE PART TO PLAY IN THIS DRAMA! Every one of us has issues, things we struggle with and hopefully are working through. Take a look at all the things you wrote above. What is God trying to say *to* you?

4 a.) What do you think He is trying to *do in* you?

4 b.) When the Lord does great things IN you, he can do great things THROUGH you. What do you think God wants to do *through* you, both in your life and ministry to the Lord and to others?

5.) Allow God to work in your life. What are some things you can be decisive and pro-active in right now as you engage the opportunities and challenges presented above?

6.) When you become intimate with the love of your life, you will let go of the things that may displease him or her. When you truly come close to God, you come close to His glory. And when you do that, you have to let go of whatever displeases Him: thoughts, deeds, habits, mannerisms, everything...

Hollywood, business people, the media—many voices are constantly trying to inject our lives with the idea that we are missing out on their version of "the good life." Moses "had it all" for the first and formative part of his life, yet he gladly left it behind permanently.

Why is it so easy to fall prey to these seductions?

We are all "human." Could it be that we enjoy some things that God has clearly shown are actually to our detriment? Why?

7.) *"Then they said to Moses, 'You speak with us, and we will hear; but let not God speak with us, lest we die.' And Moses said to the people, 'Do not fear; for God has come to test you, and that His fear may be before you, so that you may not sin.' So the people stood afar off, but Moses drew near the thick darkness where God was.'* —Exodus 20:19-21

"They stay away from the light for fear of their sins will be exposed." —John 3:20, NLT

There is a struggle. Typically, we don't want to confront the sin that we may still embrace or be bound in or even enjoy. Have you ever been reluctant to hear God's voice when it lays bare the condition of your heart? _____

8.) Things kept secret probably won't be confronted. Have you ever been concerned that if you draw too close to the Lord something may be revealed that you want to remain secret? _____

Everybody wants to know the secret! Or do they?

9.) *"The secret [of the sweet, satisfying companionship] of the Lord have they who fear (revere and worship) Him, and He will show them His covenant and reveal to them its [deep, inner] meaning."* —Psalm 25:14, Amplified

"And Moses said to the people, 'Do not fear; for God has come to test you, and that His fear may be before you, so that you may not sin.'" —Exodus 20:20 NIV

In session three you saw a paradox, something that was seemingly contradictory but was nonetheless true: Those who walk in deepest intimacy with Christ and become the most blessed servants of God seem to be the very ones who fear God the most! **Here we see it again: Moses says, "Hey, everybody, don't fear! 'Cause God wants to see if His fear is in you!"**

What is going on? Which is it? What is God saying here? Let's dig a little, seek the Holy Spirit's wisdom, and use our heads and hearts in the Word.

 Here is a transforming truth: There is a difference between being scared of God and the fear of God.

Look at Deuteronomy, the fifth chapter. **From God's point of view, the reason the children of Israel <u>couldn't</u> come near the Lord was because of their <u>lack</u> of the fear of Him.**

"So it was, when you heard the voice from the midst of the darkness, while the mountain was burning with fire, that you came near to me, all the heads of your tribes and your elders. And you said: 'Surely the LORD our God has shown us His glory and His greatness, and we have heard His voice from the midst of the fire. We have seen this day that God speaks with man; yet he still lives. Now therefore, why should we die? For this great fire will consume us; if we hear the voice of the LORD our God anymore, then we shall die. For who is there of all flesh who has heard the voice of the living God speaking from the midst of the fire, as we have, and lived? You go near and hear all that the LORD our God may say, and tell us all that the LORD our God says to you, and we will hear and do it.' Then the LORD heard the voice of your words when you spoke to me, and the LORD said to me: 'I have heard the voice of the words of this people which they have spoken to you. They are right in all that they have spoken. Oh, that they had such a heart in them that they would fear Me and always keep all My commandments, that it might be well with them and with their children forever! Go and say to them, "Return to your tents."'"
—Deuteronomy 5:23-30

The people were indeed afraid. Was the kind of fear they were experiencing the kind of fear God wants from His children? Why or why not?

10.)   Are we to be afraid of someone we are to be intimate with? The point is, God is not just "someone." And further, we are not talking about fear in the traditional, human, more negative sense. Yes, we should be afraid, very afraid—even full of terror—of the consequences of a life that doesn't fear God, a life that is lived in sin destined to be subject to the wrath of a holy, pure God. But there is another side to this coin, too. Fearing God is a love-response to our Creator. It is our awe, reverence, and adoration of the God who is so incomprehensibly powerful, yet He cares for, loves, and thinks upon us. It is our abject humility to His revealed truth! Fear of the Lord, honoring Him as God, is actually the door to intimacy with Him. Psalm 111:10 says, *"The fear of the LORD is the* beginning of wisdom; a good understanding have all those who do His commandments." Why wouldn't God have said "love" Him instead of fear Him in Deuteronomy 5:29?

11.) Exodus 20:20 says, "*God has come to test you, and that His fear may be before you, so that you may not sin.*" It is the fear of the Lord that keeps us from sin, not the love of God.

How is it that our fear of God keeps us from sin?

12.) There is a difference between being ___*scared*___ of God and the

___*fear*___ of the Lord. The person who is _____ of God has

something to _____. He runs from the presence of the Lord.

This is just what the people of Israel were doing in the above passage. When Adam sinned in Genesis, he ran from the Lord. These examples show the spirit of fear. God has not given us that.

But the person who fears God and has nothing to hide actually is afraid of being

___*away*___ **from God.** And that is what keeps us from sin.

13.) Is it possible to "love Jesus" and still not fear God? Explain.

14.)   What are the two great forces that keep us on the road of life?

1. _____

2. _____

In the New Testament God is called both Abba Father (love) and Consuming Fire (fear). How is it possible that He is both to us?

What are some ways in which each keeps us on the road of life?
- Love: Father/Daddy/God

- Fear: Consuming fire

15.)   To fear God means you will _____ what He loves.

You will _____ what He hates.

What is _____ to Him is important to you.

The manifestation of the fear of the Lord is always to keep all of His _____. (See Deuteronomy 5:29.)

"We have to have a reformation, which means a change of the way we view things and do things when it comes to our having an intimate relationship with God."

—John Bevere

What fire has God lit in your heart today? To finish this session, prayerfully write your thoughts on what the statement above might mean. First in your life, in your personal mission:

And in the church as a whole:

A HEART ABLAZE, IGNITING A PASSION FOR GOD

Mission Five

The prophet Isaiah said this in Isaiah 44:10: *"Who would form a god or mold an image that profits him nothing?"*

MISSION: CONFRONTATION BRINGS TRANSFORMATION TODAY

"Then it came to pass on the third day, in the morning, that there were thunderings and lightnings, and a thick cloud on the mountain; and the sound of the trumpet was very loud, so that all the people who were in the camp trembled. And Moses brought the people out of the camp to meet with God, and they stood at the foot of the mountain. Now Mount Sinai was completely in smoke, because the LORD descended upon it in fire. Its smoke ascended like the smoke of a furnace, and the whole mountain quaked greatly." —Exodus 19:16-18

"And God spoke all these words, saying: 'I am the LORD your God, who brought you out of the land of Egypt, out of the house of bondage.'" —Exodus 20:1

1.) True/False: Coming out of Egypt, the people of Israel had enjoyed God's miracles and provision (prosperity, healing, deliverance, etc.) and seemed ready to meet God in His glory. Yet when they had the chance to experience God in His glory as Moses had, they refused.

In Deuteronomy 5 God even tells Moses that the people were correct—essentially they were not prepared to meet God, and they would be consumed.

In Matthew 7:20-23 Jesus said, *"Therefore by their fruits you will know them. Not everyone who says to Me, 'Lord, Lord,' shall enter the kingdom of heaven, but he who does the will of My Father in heaven. Many will say to Me in that day, 'Lord, Lord, have we not prophesied in Your name, cast out demons in Your name, and done many wonders in Your name?' And then I will declare to them, 'I never knew you; depart from Me, you who practice lawlessness!'"*

How do Jesus' words relate to the account of the people of Israel (in Exodus and Deuteronomy) and to us today?

2.) True/False: We're to cleanse ourselves from the filth of the garments of the flesh and spirit in preparation for God's coming glory.

3.) Regarding your role in holiness and sanctification, explain the following statement: "God supplies the ability; you are the one who is to do it."

4.) In Exodus 19, the people of Israel ran from the presence of God because sin cannot hide in the presence of God's glory. In this chapter, as well as when Jesus walked the earth, we see miracles all around God's people, and they were comfortable with it. Yet there was tremendous iniquity in their hearts. When God's glory comes, however, sin is going to be revealed. Read the account of Ananias and Sapphira in Acts, chapter 5, and explain how their story relates to this.

syn·o·nym (sin´ə nim), *n.* a word having the same or nearly the same meaning as another in the language.

Finney and the Fear of God Were Synonymous

Few people have influenced the subject of revival like **Charles G. Finney** (1792-1875). He was bold and brilliant, calculating and controversial, and has been considered the father of modern revivalism. No one can argue with his genuine results. In difficult times he saw more than 500,000 conversions in his ministry, before there were amplifiers and mass communication. In many ways Finney paved the path for the mass evangelists who would come after him—people like Dwight L. Moody, Billy Sunday, and Billy Graham.

With an emphasis on the believer's personal responsibility in holiness, Finney removed a lot of excuses for a lax lifestyle. *"Christian perfection is a duty,"* he taught. *"This is evident from the fact that God requires it, both in the law and under the gospel. The command in the text 'be ye therefore perfect, as your father in heaven is perfect' is given under the gospel. If anyone contends that the gospel requires less holiness than the law, I would ask him to say just how much less it requires."*[5]

Although Finney knew the grace and power of the Holy Spirit, and certainly understood the Spirit's role in the church better than most, he also felt the believer had a bigger part to play in his or her own holiness than the church often taught. See if this excerpt sets *your* heart ablaze:

"Too long has the church been in the habit of thinking that the great design of the gospel is to save men from the punishment of sin; whereas its real design is to deliver men from sin. But Christians have taken the other ground and think of nothing but that they are to go on in sin; and all they hope for is to be forgiven, and when they die to be made holy in heaven. Oh, if they only realized that the whole framework of the gospel is designed to break the power of sin and fill men on earth with all the fullness of God, how soon there would be one steady blaze of love in the hearts of God's people all over the world!"[6]

Finney once said (paraphrased), "In revivals I have known God to do some terrible things in righteousness."[7]

Following is a riveting account of God's dealings in one of the young Finney's very first revivals.

"There was an old man in this place, who was not only an infidel, but a great railer at religion. He was very angry at the revival movement. I heard every day of his railing and blaspheming, but took no public notice of it. He refused altogether to attend meetings. But in the midst of his opposition, and when his excitement was great, while sitting one morning at the table, he suddenly fell out of his chair in a fit of apoplexy. A physician was immediately called, who, after a brief examination, told him that he could live but a short time; and that if he had anything to say, he must say it at once. He had just enough strength and time, as I was informed, to stammer out, 'Don't let Finney pray over my corpse.' This was the last of his opposition in that place."[8]

How does this revival story resemble Ananias and Sapphira's story? **Also,** could this man and Ananias and Sapphira have possibly made better choices?

5.) God wanted to embrace the children of Israel as a loving Father, but they ran from Him instead of to Him. In what ways is God revealed as a father in the Scriptures?

In what ways has He revealed himself to you as a father?

Now make it really personal. In what ways would you like to see God *further* reveal Himself to you as a loving heavenly Father? (As you write this, recall your personal mission statement from the first session.)

REACHING OUT

6.) *"Thus, by their fruit you will recognize them. Not everyone who says to me, 'Lord, Lord,' will enter the kingdom of heaven, but only he who does the will of my Father who is in heaven."* Matthew 7:20-21, NIV.

God is working *in* you to produce the fruit of righteousness, and He also desires to work *through* you to reach others. In the last session you recorded ways you felt God desired to work through you. How can you be a vessel God would flow through? **Record here some ways you could let God flow through you, showing the characteristics of the love of the Father** (see question #5 above) **to a generation of people who desperately need to know Him.** Think in terms of meeting people's practical physical needs *and* spiritual needs. A bag of groceries, an encouraging word, or a personal word of prayer can go a long way to showing someone that there is a Father God.

It has been said that the road to hell is paved with good intentions. The verse in Matthew 7 shows the truth to that.

Loving our neighbor as ourselves is not something to just talk about or dream about. We can pray and give God the opportunity to really speak to us and flow through us. This is different from our first "Reaching Out" experience. This time you want to specifically reach out to someone who is broken or downtrodden.

Here's an example: Ethel was a 63-year-old woman who had been abandoned by a drunken husband. She had little money and a poor apartment to live in. She had taken in her unsaved teenage niece, who was a real handful. Ethel worked long hard hours as a check-out person in a supermarket. She had to walk and take the bus to get there and back. Along with several physical and medical problems, she was depressed. Yet she always tried to keep her head up, keep pressing forward, serve in her church, and raise her niece according to God's word. Despite her tireless efforts, Ethel was always behind on her expenses, always in need of a way to church, always under difficult pressures, and in need of many things. Truly she was a person with abundant opportunity for the right people to hear from God and bless her with things such as prayer, encouragement, a ride to church, furnishings for her apartment, food, help with her niece, etc.

There is need all around us—we cannot be God, nor can we be everybody's care-taker. But we ARE called to hear from God and to reach out. Is there an Ethel or someone like her in your life?

Write here one name of someone you will *pray for* on a regular basis as the Holy Spirit brings him or her to mind; be open to meeting some physical needs, too (food, clothing, a ride to church, a Bible, cleaning or painting for them, an encouraging note with a gift certificate, etc.).

Name: _____

This is a simple challenge you can easily fulfill. Don't let it be a one-time, now-you-are-done-and-have-eased-your-conscience type of exercise. As the Lord transforms our lives, being led by Him to reach out to others should be our very lifestyle. Take some time, and enjoy hearing from God. Let this flow from the Holy Spirit, and see how He leads you to make a lasting impact on this person or situation. Perhaps you might even enlist the help of others as the Lord leads you.

7.) Just because someone is gifted as a leader doesn't mean he or she is blessed by God or in God's will. Hitler was a gifted but perverted leader. People have built large churches and ministries only to fall miserably when God exposes sin. In what ways do you think the people of God would be protected if we would learn this truth?

8.) ⊙ **A manageable deity** ⊙

"Now when the people saw that Moses delayed coming down from the mountain, the people gathered together to Aaron, and said to him, 'Come, make us gods that shall go before us; for as for this Moses, the man who brought us up out of the land of Egypt, we do not know what has become of him.' And Aaron said to them, 'Break off the golden earrings which are in the ears of your wives, your sons, and your daughters, and bring them to me.' So all the people broke off the golden earrings which were in their ears, and brought them to Aaron. And he received the gold from their hand, and he fashioned it with an engraving tool, and made a molded calf. Then they said, 'This is your god, O Israel, that brought you out of the land of Egypt!' So when Aaron saw it, he built an altar before it. And Aaron made a proclamation and said, 'Tomorrow is a feast to the LORD.'"
—Exodus 32:1-5

Aaron actually beheld the golden calf he'd fashioned and in essence proclaimed it the one true God. He led the people as they worshiped it as the very God Jehovah who brought them out of Egypt.

What is the significance of this?

9.) Aaron had not been on top of the mountain. He hadn't beheld God for forty days and nights as Moses did. For eighty-three years, Aaron had been raised in Egypt. He grew up with all kinds of these images around. These images were a reflection of the gods that they served. Aaron was used to this.

What is the result of this? What is the truth at the very heart of this message?

Aaron's inward _____ of God (*Yahweh*) was _____ by the

society in which he was raised; therefore, that's what came out of him: an idol. In this

case the golden calf.

10.)

Be bold, be adventurous. Go where few others dare to go: To glory!

Our society doesn't worship images of insects or calves or such. We worship "self." It is our own selves we have exalted and pursued with all our energies and passion.

- The daily emphasis on wealth and success in business and careers
- Our obsession with sex in movies, music, magazines and advertising
- The fact that millions of people are heavily in debt on credit cards

…these are all signs of our obsession with ourselves.

Think hard, as this affects your very soul. List here several other examples of our society's obsession and worship of self; what do you see all around you, daily, in contemporary society?

11.) How may have you fallen into the traps of some of the things in question #10?

Confronting these will gloriously transform your life!

The answers to that question will give you some insight into this next question.

Read the following verses and think about them. It all falls into place and starts making perfect sense.

Isaiah the prophet said this: *"Who would form a god or mold an image that profits him nothing?"* —Isaiah 44:10

The apostle Paul put it this way: *"We told you about Jesus, and you received the Holy Spirit and accepted our message. But you let some people tell you about another Jesus. Now you are ready to receive another spirit and accept a different message."* —2 Corinthians 11:4, Contemporary English Version

Idols give their creator whatever their creator wants. That is why we so easily fall into false worship. It serves us well, telling us what we want to hear and allowing us to do what we want to do, but still satisfying our inborn need to worship.

The contemporary church often echoes the world. We create a Jesus that blesses, heals, prospers, promotes, and smooth-talks, but we forget the weightier matters of God's reality: His holiness, His demand for obedience, His majesty, sovereignty, fear, and other divine attributes that challenge our selfish nature. His blessings are to be the fruit of our relationship with Him, not the object of our worship.

Certainly not all life's answers are easy or the same for everyone. But just as certainly we can justify anything and any lifestyle with our own spiritual-sounding rationalization and the false Jesus we tell ourselves is the real Jesus. How we live regarding divorce, abortion, sex, money, politics, education, the way we raise our children, the church we attend, our taxes—the list is as long as there are diverse kinds of people and desires.

Take a moment to gather your thoughts. Think back to your personal mission statement. **Transformation** and **the glory of a changed life** is the mission. Relax and ask God's assistance and presence. **It is time to be very serious and ask God to truly reveal to you your own motives and your own heart. Don't make the mistake of thinking "not me" before you have even considered what the Lord is saying here.**

Is it possible that you are serving or have served a Jesus whose image you have created? A Jesus formed in your imagination? (Notice the word *image* is within the word *imagination*.)

In what ways might you be serving a God who tends only to tell you *what you want to hear and always seems to give you your desires?*

12.) Is your inward image of Jesus shaped by the society in which you live? How can you escape? We haven't the power to free *ourselves* from all of society's traps or from our own selfish rebellion and delusions. But we *can cooperate* with the Holy Spirit, and God's Word can set us free. We may have to make some tough decisions and leave some things behind, but we *can* worship the God who is seated at the right hand of our heavenly Father—Jesus Christ as He really is, not as we want him to be to suit our selfishness.

What can this mean to you? How can you see God helping you change your understanding of Him?

13.) How will this change your relationship with Him?

14.) Can you see some ways the Holy Spirit can help you make good decisions, wise choices that will both disentangle you from the world and keep you from being further poisoned by false conceptions of who God really is?

15.) Read this life-challenging statement:

"It's very simple, folks; one of two things is going to happen in the life of a believer. Either they're going to conform into the image of Jesus by the fear of the Lord, or they are going to conform Jesus into the image of what they desire. So, it's very simple: if you go to the mountain, you change. If you stay at the foot, like Aaron, and play church, God's image in you changes."

—John Bevere

This can be a holy, solemn time. Journal here your thoughts and meditations about this message. What are you struggling with? What is God saying? Are you sure? It's OK to be unsure. You are working out your salvation with fear and trembling, joyful at the prospect of pleasing the real Jesus of the Bible. Don't be afraid to bare your heart and soul. Let the Holy Spirit and God's written Word transform you in a way that brings lasting glory to Him and to your life.

Date: _____

A HEART ABLAZE, IGNITING A PASSION FOR GOD

Mission Six

Romans 12:2 says *"And do not be conformed to this world, but be transformed by the renewing of your mind, that you may prove what is that good and acceptable and perfect will of God."*

MISSION: IDENTIFY THE CORE MOTIVATION OF YOUR LIFE

conform (kən-fôrm´), *v.i.* to reduce to a likeness in manners, opinions, or moral qualities. *Suschematizo* (Greek), meaning to fashion or shape one thing like another.

"And he received the gold from their hand, and he fashioned it with an engraving tool, and made a molded calf. Then they said, 'This is your god, O Israel, that brought you out of the land of Egypt!' So when Aaron saw it, he built an altar before it. And Aaron made a proclamation and said, 'Tomorrow is a feast to the LORD.'" —Exodus 32:4-5

1.) Read the definitions of the word *conform*. How does it apply to what Aaron and the people of Israel did in Exodus 32

2.) _____ is the motivating factor of a human being. We will always

_____ its course.

3.) *"But every man is tempted, when he is drawn away of his own lust, and enticed."*
—James 1:14, KJV
"But each one is tempted when he is drawn away by his own desires and enticed."
—James 1:14, NKJV

Many times people confuse their _____ with their _____.
Often we intend to do things but end up going the way of our desires instead.

TRANSFORMED WITHIN

"For it is God who works in you both to will and to do for His good pleasure." Philippians 2:13

The *inner conflict!*

You can have very good or godly intentions, but they may not be your true desires.
This is a sobering and very important fact as well as being a key component of this session's message. The statement reveals a tremendous source of *inner conflict* we all have to some degree.

The Gospels contain several accounts of those who came to Jesus intending to follow Him (like the rich young ruler in Luke 18), but when Jesus confronted the true desires within them, they drew back.

Today we have seen movie stars, pop music stars, the wealthy, and the powerful profess salvation and then fall away. We seem to understand these instances, because these people have so much of the world's riches. At times it seems (wrongly) that we can almost justify their choice, because of the tremendous pull all the pleasures of the world have for them.

But the conflict of desires and intentions—following Christ versus our inner desires—is certainly not limited to the rich and powerful.

A missionary story (paraphrased)
A reporter asked a renowned yet humble godly missionary, "In all your world travels, of all the people you've met these very many years, who are those you find to be the godliest—the rich or the poor?" Everyone was astonished when the missionary said, "The rich." Incredulous at the reply, the reporter responded, "The rich—how can that be?"

"Why," replied the great missionary, "multitudes of the world's poor intensely desire to find relief and happiness in riches. The rich have often found the terrible truth of the emptiness of their wealth and have learned to find solace in Christ alone."

4.) What is the point that story is making?

What does it mean to you?

5.) **It is actually true!** The truth *will* set you free, but first you must face it.

For the rich young ruler, it was his fine things in life. For some it is relationships; for others it is security. It is *our own desires* and lusts that the devil uses to entice us. It doesn't necessarily matter where these came from in our lives. What matters is that they exist and have a hold on us.

Has this study so far revealed any areas of conflict within you that you'd never felt or been aware of before? Whatever your place in life, ponder how this message is playing out within you. **What conflict of worldly and sinful desires, lusts, habits, or attitudes can you see at work within you that are against the will of Christ?** Another way to put it is this: What things do you inwardly desire that would grieve the Holy Spirit and are against the Word of God?

6.) Can you see any ways in which following the course of your own desires could eventually cause you to walk away from God—perhaps even sadly and sorrowfully as the rich ruler did—*but walking away nonetheless*?

7.) There is great hope for each of us, no matter our wrong desires or challenges! What is God's remedy to this conflict?

8.) *"And those who are Christ's have crucified the flesh with its passions and desires. If we live in the Spirit, let us also walk in the Spirit."* —Galatians 5:24-25

Many today confuse verses 24 and 25 of Galatians the fifth chapter. They believe that it is saying the Spirit crucifies the flesh and its passions. Is it the Spirit, or is it our responsibility to crucify the lusts of our flesh? What is the accurate understanding of these two verses?

9.) In session 5, we looked at the life of Charles Finney. Read this excerpt again:

" Too long has the church been in the habit of thinking that the great design of the gospel is to save men from the punishment of sin; whereas its real design is to deliver men from sin. But Christians have taken the other ground and think of nothing but that they are to go on in sin; and all they hope for is to be forgiven, and when they die to be made holy in heaven. Oh, if they only realized that the whole framework of the gospel is designed to break the power of sin and fill men on earth with all the fullness of God, how soon there would be one steady blaze of love in the hearts of God's people all over the world!" —Charles G. Finney

Although it was written over 150 years ago, it is remarkably in sync with *A Heart Ablaze*. How does it compare to what you have been learning?

Comment on the critical distinction made in the first sentence: *" Too long has the church been in the habit of thinking that the great design of the gospel is to save men from the punishment of sin; whereas its real design is to deliver men* from *sin.* What is the difference between salvation from *the punishment of sin* and being *delivered from* sin?

"You have loved righteousness and hated lawlessness; therefore God, Your God, has anointed You with the oil of gladness more than Your companions." —Hebrews 1:9

Personal application, genuine transformation is our mission. *It's the point of all this.* The reason many are not set free is because we strongly desire things that are sinful. But God blesses those who love righteousness and hate sin. How does it change the way you perceive life when you take in the glorious truth that God didn't go through all this just to keep you from missing the punishment of hell? He gave His life for you so you could really be FREE from sin—the very sin that has plagued and tormented and continually frustrated you!

Journal here the way this truth makes you feel. Are you empowered? Some have said it makes them feel hopeful and inspired—ready to do some soul-searching and changing. Others feel "on top of the world"—they think of being on a beautiful mountaintop or surfing a majestic wave or beholding a valley full of colorful wildflowers with a refreshing spring running through it. All of these actually are very biblical images. People tend to say they feel a burden lifted so they can move forward with the Lord like never before. Still others have been moved to fast and pray. You can be free *right now*—let God speak in all His glory. What does this mean to YOU?

Now ask God to show you any specific <u>action(s)</u> you must take to live this out; to be free from wrong desires, lusts, and any sins that have held you. Journal here, date it, and FOLLOW THROUGH on what The Lord shows you.

Date: _____

"The reason we're not seeing a stronger anointing in our churches is because people still have a strong desire for sin. See, this is what happens when you come into God's presence; He exposes these things. And this is what we've got to be willing to do. We have to be willing to say, 'Let the cross slay it.'"

—John Bevere

10.) In today's church you see two different types of people—some like Moses, and some like Israel. What is the difference between the two types of people?

11.)   **Moses chose God** over God's promises.

"By faith Moses, when he became of age, refused to be called the son of Pharaoh's daughter, choosing rather to suffer affliction with the people of God than to enjoy the passing pleasures of sin, esteeming the reproach of Christ greater riches than the treasures in Egypt; for he looked to the reward. By faith he forsook Egypt, not fearing the wrath of the king; for he endured as seeing Him who is invisible." —Hebrews 11:24-27

The people of Israel were very willing to live with God's blessings and promises, regardless of whether or not God Himself was present. When Moses, however, was given the choice, he actually told the Lord, *"If Your presence does not go with us, do not bring us up from here."*

Sometimes God will present us with choices, even what are seemingly blessings, expecting us to choose the right thing.

Has this ever happened in your life? Was there a job you really wanted, more money, a better location? Or perhaps it was a ministry opportunity or someone you desired to be with, and it seemed harmless, a great blessing, and a desire of your heart. You wanted to and could have said "yes." But you knew God's Word, and you felt His Spirit really desired something that was much better for you—His presence, His delight that you chose the right thing. So you refused the desire and instead felt the incomparable thrill of God's ultimate blessing: not some new job or some such thing, but His very presence! Has this happened in your life? Like Moses, your reward was not the Promised Land, but the promiser Himself—the One from whom all promises flow anyway! What could be better?

Is this the case in any area of your life at this moment? Is God asking you to choose His presence over something you desire? Write about it below.

12.) **Focus** helps you chart your course.

"I press toward the goal for the prize of the upward call of God in Christ Jesus." —Philippians 3:14

The great men and women of the Bible kept their eyes focused on God, not just His blessings. But the children of Israel constantly dug themselves deeper into the mire of their own selfishness and disobedience! Taking some quality time now to discern God's will for your life will save you lots of trouble later! Not all things are obviously harmful, sinful desires, but their dangers are more subtle.

Are there things in your life that may be preventing you from focusing on God? It's easy to take our gaze off of the Lord and be distracted by "harmless" blessings instead. TV, movies, relationships, purchasing that new, bigger, better home, car or boat, or that big screen TV, etc. Even hobbies or church work can steer us off course. Sometimes God would have us just be content *without* some things, being happy as we are, simply with His presence. *"Godliness with contentment is great gain"* (1 Timothy 6:6).

Examine your heart. Are there some things in front of you currently that may not seem so bad? Let God shed His light on those things, and you'll see if you are on the path of life or if you should make some adjustments. Write any distractions *and* the adjustments you'll make:

13.) **The whole focus comes down to the core motivation for the lives of Moses and Israel.**
- The core motivation for Moses' life was that he loved God for who He is.
- The core motivation for Israel was that they loved God for what He could do for them.

Before you began *A Heart Ablaze*, which category did you fall into?

Why do you say that?

14.) At this point, this very moment, you are probably dealing with many thoughts and emotions. Which category did you feel you are in AT THIS MOMENT?

Why?

15.) Which category do you *want* to be in? Remember—the road to hell is paved with good intentions. Don't just answer these questions glibly, off-handedly, with no thought of God or the consequences of your motives or actions. This is a serious transformation we are talking about, and you can and must choose well. The Holy Spirit is moving to help you. *Write your musings with all seriousness of purpose, and follow through with God's leading:*

At the beginning, in our first session, we talked about life's greatest achievers, those in business, sports, etc., who had a written mission and fulfilled it. Did you know that just the fact that you wrote down your Personal Mission Statement for *A Heart Ablaze* puts you in the very top percentage of people everywhere? And completing this workbook puts you in an even higher percentile!

You are a rare breed because you are taking steps 95 percent of all people only talk about!

Be encouraged! God IS at work within you, and He WILL complete the good work He has begun in you!

A HEART ABLAZE, IGNITING A PASSION FOR GOD

Mission Seven

Romans 12:1 in the Amplified Version of the Bible says *"I appeal to you therefore, brethren, and beg of you in view of [all] the mercies of God, to* **make a decisive dedication** *of your* **bodies** *[presenting all your members and faculties] as a living sacrifice, holy (devoted, consecrated) and well pleasing to God, which is your* **reasonable (rational, intelligent) service and spiritual worship"** *(emphasis added).*

MISSION: CHOOSE TO DEVELOP A STRONG SPIRIT SO YOU CAN CONTROL ATMOSPHERES.

"If you're stronger in God than the sinner is in their sin, then you will control the atmosphere."

—John Bevere

1.) Why are "atmospheres" important in our Christian walk?

our sroundings - we can choose our atmosphere

2.) 🔹 **The results of our life's decisions** 🔹

We've all heard the simple but meaningful adage *"Don't put the cart before the horse."* But in today's too fast-paced society it is too easy to simply get up day after day and "do life," the usual, normal, same daily "stuff." Before you know it, YEARS have passed. *But have you put things in their proper order?* If not, you are going nowhere—and fast.

This is especially true in the things of God. *Our entire life's outcome depends on the priorities **we choose** daily. If we want God to flow through us to change and control atmospheres, we have to put first things first.*

This is crucial. Allow your heart the opportunity to grasp that concept for a moment. To facilitate that, we'll start with something easy: Have your parents or someone you are close with ever made a decision that cost them dearly? Or perhaps made some decisions that were a blessing? Without using any names, record the impact of their decisions, good or poor, had on them and those dear to them:

3.) It's relatively easy to see these things in others, but how about yourself? What decisions have you made that cost you in some way in your life?

Or blessed you?

4.)   How may those decisions have affected others?

_____

5.)   Going back in time to set things in order might seem to be a great temptation. While that is not reality, this is: **You can make wise choices from now on!** Think of it this way:

You can CHOOSE to make right choices! You have learned a lot about getting set free from Egypt and getting Egypt out of you. Look what Joshua told the people of Israel about choosing:

"And if it seems evil to you to serve the LORD, choose for yourselves this day whom you will serve, whether the gods which your fathers served that were on the other side of the River, or the gods of the Amorites, in whose land you dwell. But as for me and my house, we will serve the LORD." —Joshua 24:15

We have a choice, and if we are saved, we have the Holy Spirit within us helping us make the *correct* choice. It is important to remember, though: **The Holy Spirit does not do the choosing of what or whom to serve; YOU do.** God has given you awesome responsibility. God is trusting that you will choose wisely. The fact that you are on this *Ablaze* mission shows God is teaching and leading you to those right decisions in all areas of your life!

This mission is revealing the influence of today's society and culture on our lives. It can be startling how subtle the world can be when it comes to infiltrating *your* Christian life!

As you have completed these sessions, in what ways are you progressing *from ignorance or a passive attitude* of what things are sinful *to a knowledge* of sin?

_____

6.) "So, this is what God's people should desire. We should not desire to be conformed to the patterns of this world, but transformed into God's way of living."

—John Bevere

"Scandalous behavior is rapidly destroying American Christianity. By their daily activity most 'Christians' regularly commit treason. With their mouths they claim that Jesus is Lord, but with their actions they demonstrate allegiance to money, sex and self-fulfillment."
—Ron Sider, "The Scandal of the Evangelical Conscience," www.christianitytoday.com

"George Gallup and Barna hand us survey after survey demonstrating that evangelical Christians are as likely to embrace lifestyles every bit as hedonistic, materialistic, self centered and sexually immoral as the world in general."
—Theologian Michael Horton, in Sider, "The Scandal of the Evangelical Conscience," www.christianitytoday.com

"Every day the church is becoming more like the world it allegedly seeks to change."
—George Barna, in Sider, "The Scandal of the Evangelical Conscience," www.christianitytoday.com

"Our research has shown that most of the influences on what people think and do come from just seven sources: Movies, television, music, family, books, law and the internet. That same body of research shows that the local church has virtually no discernible influence on people's lives."
—George Barna, *New Directions*

Are the voices of society and popular culture telling us what to buy, what to value, and how to live? Are they shaping our lives, or is the Word of God? How and why?

Clothing, entertainment, music, media, career goals, family values, money/giving, sexual relationships, etc: **Does the church of today move with the current of the world's culture, or does it hold to its own counterculture with a biblical standard?**

 7.)   History Makers

"The god of this age has blinded the minds of unbelievers, so that they cannot see the light of the gospel of the glory of Christ, who is the image of God." —2 Corinthians 4:4, NIV

 The Funeral of Your Own Independence!

There is a battle going on! When you choose to serve God and walk in His ways, you receive God's light. You get God's revelation, from His Word, of who He really is! Your eyes are opened, and the blinders of Satan come off and the intoxication of the worlds system grows weaker and weaker. Having transformed you within, God can really begin to work in your life to transform the lives of others. You can be a blessing and make a real difference in people's lives! But remember—you have to put first things first.

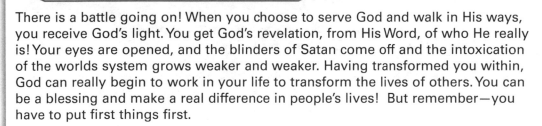

*"The battle is lost or won in the secret places of the will before God, never first in the external world. . . . Every now and again, not often, but sometimes, God brings us to a point of climax. That is the Great Divide in the life; **from that point we either go towards a more and more dilatory and useless type of Christian life, or we become more and more <u>ablaze</u> for the glory of God**—[Our] Utmost for His Highest."* —Oswald Chambers, *My Utmost For His Highest* (in the original English), excerpts from day 12/27 (emphasis added)

Oswald Chambers (1874-1917) was a man who well understood the inner turmoil that occurs when faced with choosing God or self. Constantly praised for his artistic, intellectual, and ministry gifts, he struggled deeply with his own conflict regarding career choices, his own sinfulness, and God's desires for his life. Ultimately Chambers chose to forsake many things that fought for the throne of his heart, including promising careers and a deep friendship of eight years with a Christian woman whom he might have instead married. It was later said he cared not for money or personal advantage or for the praises of others, but only the message God had given him.

As He does with each of us, first having transformed Chambers within, God could now transform others through him. Born in Scotland, Chambers' ministry took him to Egypt, Japan, and the United States. Much of his preaching was transcribed by his wife after his death, eventually becoming (among other books) a world-changing daily devotional entitled *My Utmost for His Highest.* The work has far eclipsed what most books ever attain to, remaining steadily in print for decades, to this day!

"Some of us are trying to offer up spiritual sacrifices to God before we have sacrificed the natural. The only way in which we can offer a spiritual sacrifice to God is by presenting our bodies a living sacrifice. Sanctification means more than deliverance from sin, it means the deliberate commitment of myself whom God has saved to God, and that I do not care what it costs."
—Oswald Chambers, *My Utmost for His Highest* (in the original English), excerpts from day 12/10

"And they that are Christ's have crucified the flesh with the affections and lusts."
—Galatians 5:24, KJV

"It is not a question of giving up sin, but of giving up my right to myself, my natural independence and self-assertiveness, and this is where the battle has to be fought. Very few of us debate with the sordid and evil and wrong, but we do debate with the good. It is the good that hates the best, and the higher up you get in the scale of the natural virtues, the more intense is the opposition to Jesus Christ. "They that are Christ's have crucified the flesh" - it is going to cost the natural in you everything, not something. Jesus said, "If any man will be My disciple, let him deny himself," i.e., his right to himself, and a man has to realize Who Jesus Christ is before he will do it. Beware of refusing to go to the funeral of your own independence.".
—Oswald Chambers, *My Utmost for His Highest* (in the original English), excerpts from day 12/9

Oswald Chambers spoke eloquently of the struggle of self and sin versus godliness. Have you mixed some of the things of the world in with God?

Are there some specific things God has been revealing to you, *perhaps things that maybe you had not viewed as sin but now you are coming to a new realization of God's standards and desires for you*? What are those specific areas?

8.) Our daily lives can cause us to be surrounded with unrighteousness. Yet because it is our mission field, we are protected and not tormented or vexed, but we can be as shining beacons of God's light.

What is the important difference between your work versus participation in certain things of the world's culture, such as movies, music, or more subtle things such as attitudes about money, relationships, self-fulfillment, etc.?

9.) **A forever** life-changing principle!

Wrong choices of friends, movies, music; strife and complaining...this is not the atmosphere where the Spirit of God delights to dwell. Instead, create an atmosphere that the Spirit of God would delight to dwell in—in your home, family, job, and life. How can you do this?

10.) The early church was persecuted because they had a lifestyle that was "counterculture," as opposed to "sub-culture." What is the difference?

11.) The world today is often upset with the church for very different reasons. What are these, and why are they not good reasons?

12.) How has the atmosphere in today's church often tended to create a sub-culture instead of a counterculture?

13.) Holiness transcends such legalism as rules for dress or hair or what and when to eat. If you are living a holy lifestyle, you will automatically want to do things in a way that glorifies the Lord. It could be described as adopting God's ____ *ways* ____ and coming up to His level of ____ *living* ____ .

14.) ⬧ **Decision Time** ⬧

> **re·nounce** (ri nouns´), *v.*, **1.** to give up, especially by formal announcement. **2.** to reject or disown.

"Rather, we have renounced secret and shameful ways; we do not use deception, nor do we distort the word of God. On the contrary, by setting forth the truth plainly we commend ourselves to every man's conscience in the sight of God."
—2 Corinthians 4:2, NIV

"Abstain from evil [shrink from it and keep aloof from it] in whatever form or whatever kind it may be."
—1 Thessalonians 5:22, Amplified Bible

"He who conceals his sins does not prosper, but whoever confesses and renounces them finds mercy."
—Proverbs 28:13, NIV

Are you ready for some of God's great mercy in your life as you are being transformed more into His image? Now is the time to renounce any and all sins, strongholds, or sinful desires. Scripture is clear—God will forgive you and transform you as you repent, telling the Lord you are sorry and asking for help in forsaking the evil ways of the world.

- *"Repent, then, and turn to God, so that your sins may be wiped out, that times of refreshing may come from the Lord."* —Acts 3:19, NIV
- *"If we confess our sins, He is faithful and just to forgive us our sins and to cleanse us from all unrighteousness."* —1 John 1:9
- *"And the prayer offered in faith will make the sick person well; the Lord will raise him up. If he has sinned, he will be forgiven."* —James 5:15, NIV

 Here is a prayer to assist you: "Lord God, I praise You for this mission You've led me on. I need Your help. Please help me identify and turn from the sin(s) in my life."

Now take some time to review the areas of sin that you have noted in #7. Is there more to add? If there are any areas that you are not ready to leave behind, *ask the Lord to change your desires and to give you the desire to repent in those areas.*

If you are ready to repent, then pray now. Here is a simple effective prayer to help you:

"Father God, I believe in Jesus Christ, that He is the Son of God who was crucified and raised from the dead. And I believe in the Holy Spirit who has been sent to help me. I confess that I have sinned in the following ways: (List the sin[s].)

"I renounce these sins. I reject them and forsake them right now! Lord, I will no longer use my life or my body for sinful purposes. I break any power of these sins over me, in the strong name of Jesus! Forgive me, Lord, I pray right now. Cleanse me now, Father, with the blood of Jesus.

"Lord, with the help of Your Spirit, the Word of God, and strong fellow Christians, I will stay alert and watchful so that I do not allow myself to return to these sins or to be drawn into the world's ways, attitudes, entertainments, idols, sinful pleasures, and addictions. Society and culture will not rule me. You are my Lord! I will follow Your way of life. I have decided I will make the right choices, and I praise You right now for forgiving me, cleansing me, and empowering me to live as You want me to! To live holy and boldly as a witness by Your Spirit in the midst of this crooked and perverse generation! In Jesus' name I pray. Amen!"

Signed: _____

Date: _____

TRANSFORMED WITHIN

15.) "God says, 'The ones who are going to come near Me and minister to Me and see My face and be close to Me are the ones who didn't go the ways of the world.' What do you want to do? The choice is up to you."

—John Bevere

If you have chosen to repent of sin and go deeper in your Christian walk, God has forgiven you and is transforming your life. Rejoice! Journal here a summary of the choice **you have** made. Write any scripture verses the Lord has given you and any direction or revelation He has spoken to your heart today in this session. Be specific or poetic or prophetic—or however you feel moved upon by God. Let it flow from the union of your heart with His. Be sure to follow through on whatever you write.

A HEART ABLAZE, IGNITING A PASSION FOR GOD

Mission Eight

Second Corinthians 6:1 in the Amplified Bible says, *"Laboring together [as God's fellow workers] with Him then, we beg of you not to receive the grace of God in vain [that merciful kindness by which God exerts His holy influence on souls and turns them to Christ, keeping and strengthening them—do not receive it to no purpose]."*

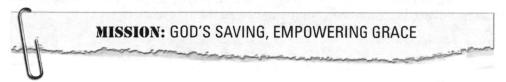

MISSION: GOD'S SAVING, EMPOWERING GRACE

1.) *"Therefore, having these promises, beloved, let us cleanse ourselves from all filthiness of the flesh and spirit, perfecting holiness in the fear of God."* —2 Corinthians 7:1

The Greek word for *perfect* is *epiteleo.* It means to "take upon one's self, to bring to an end, to accomplish, to perfect, to execute, or to complete," clarifying for us that it is our personal responsibility—not God's—to cleanse ourselves. What does 2 Corinthians 6:1 mean in context with this verse, *"We then, as workers together with Him, also plead with you not to receive the grace of God in vain"*? (Also see Amplified version above.)

2.) Describe the distorted understanding of God's grace, called "the big cover up."

3.) grace (grās), *n.*
It's your turn to provide a definition. Give the accurate definition of "grace":

4.) How could it be possible that we would see multitudes come to our altars at church services to be saved, yet we have actually deceived them?

5.) *"Therefore by their fruits you will know them. Not everyone who says to Me, 'Lord, Lord,' shall enter the kingdom of heaven, but he who does the will of My Father in heaven."* —Matthew 7:20-21

What does this verse mean in relation to question #4?

6.)   *"Think not that I am come to destroy the law, or the prophets: I am not come to destroy, but to fulfill. For verily I say unto you, Till heaven and earth pass, one jot or one tittle shall in no wise pass from the law, till all be fulfilled. Whosoever therefore shall break one of these least commandments, and shall teach men so, he shall be called the least in the kingdom of heaven: but whosoever shall do and teach them, the same shall be called great in the kingdom of heaven. For I say unto you, That except your righteousness shall exceed the righteousness of the scribes and Pharisees, ye shall in no case enter into the kingdom of heaven."* —Matthew 5:17-20, KJV

As Jesus is speaking here, what is He revealing about the gospel of grace versus the law?

7.)   If the scribes and Pharisees practiced the law seemingly without flaw, and Jesus goes on to teach that our righteousness must exceed theirs, how could anyone possibly fulfill such a lofty standard?

8.)   Matters of the Heart
Romans 8:3 in The Message declares, *"God went for the jugular when he sent his own Son. He didn't deal with the problem as something remote and unimportant. In his Son, Jesus, he personally took on the human condition, entered the disordered mess of struggling humanity in order to set it right once and for all. The law code, weakened as it always was by fractured human nature, could never have done that. The law always ended up being used as a Band-Aid on sin instead of a deep healing of it."*

Describe the life-changing difference between the outward restraining of the law versus the inward power of the Spirit.

9.) God dealt with the very heart of our sin when He sent Jesus. *"Therefore, if anyone is in Christ, he is a new creation; the old has gone, the new has come!"* —2 Corinthians 5:17, NIV

This verse in 2 Corinthians has great meaning in relation to our topic. What does it reveal about God's equipping us to obey His Word?

10.) Often people will justify ungodly lifestyles with the attitude "God knows my heart." But in Revelation, chapters two and three, Jesus repeatedly refers to people's works, not their hearts or mind's intentions. James 2:14, 18 in The Message says, *"Dear friends, do you think you'll get anywhere in this if you learn all the right words but never do anything? Does merely talking about faith indicate that a person really has it?...I can already hear one of you agreeing by saying, 'Sounds good. You take care of the faith department, I'll handle the works department'.   Not so fast. You can no more show me your works apart from your faith than I can show you my faith apart from my works. Faith and works, works and faith, fit together hand in glove."*

Describe the relationship you see here between faith and works.

11.) Impossible for man, **possible with God**

Jesus made the statement that we are known by the fruit of our lifestyles. We struggle with that because we are confronted with believing and following His Word, or consciously choosing to reject it and justify our actions. This can cause great turmoil as we wrestle with our feelings. But that is a great thing—it means the Holy Spirit is working in us! The question is whether or not we are prepared to submit our faith and our works, our very lifestyle, to Jesus in every single area.

The key is to think and believe accurately. **The gospel is good news, and we need not be overwhelmed.** Look at Jesus' disciples in Mark 10:17-27.

"Now as He was going out on the road, one came running, knelt before Him, and asked Him, 'Good Teacher, what shall I do that I may inherit eternal life?' So Jesus said to him, 'Why do you call Me good? No one is good but One, that is, God. You know the commandments: "Do not commit adultery," "Do not murder," "Do not steal," "Do not bear false witness," "Do not defraud," "Honor your father and your mother."' And he answered and said to Him, 'Teacher, all these things I have kept from my youth.' Then Jesus, looking at him, loved him, and said to him, 'One thing you lack: Go your way, sell whatever you have and give to the poor, and you will have treasure in heaven; and come, take up the cross, and follow Me.' But he was sad at this word, and went away sorrowful, for he had great possessions. Then Jesus looked around and said to His disciples, 'How hard it is for those who have riches to enter the kingdom of God!' And the disciples were astonished at His words. But Jesus answered again and said to them, 'Children, how hard it is for those who trust in riches to enter the kingdom of God! It is easier for a camel to go through the eye of a needle than for a rich man to enter the kingdom of God.' And they were greatly astonished, saying among themselves, 'Who then can be saved?' But Jesus looked at them and said, 'With men it is impossible, but not with God; for with God all things are possible.'"

Here we see a man who seemed nearly perfect, only lacking one thing. But when Jesus told him he had to change his lifestyle, he went away saddened. *He actually rejected Jesus on the spot, publicly making his choice to serve a lifestyle rather than God!*

Verse 26 shows us that even those close to Jesus were greatly astonished at how difficult it seemed to enter the kingdom of heaven. The Message puts it this way, *"That set the disciples back on their heels. 'Then who has any chance at all?' they asked."*

Put yourself in their shoes. Why do think they asked that?

If someone asked you the same questions today, how would YOU answer?

12.) "We are saved by grace and only by grace. Grace cannot be bought, it cannot be earned, you can't do enough good works to earn it. That's the first half. We've got that part down, but can I complete the story? James comes along and says, 'So, you say you've got grace, you say you got faith? Show me your grace and your faith without your works, I'll show you my grace and my faith by my works.' In other words, the evidence that I really have grace is the fact that I have a lifestyle to prove it. Because I've got God's empowering presence in me that's causing me to live the life to show it."

— John Bevere

"*Is it not evident that a person is made right with God not by a barren faith but by faith fruitful in works?*" —James 2:24, The Message

"*You see then that a man is justified by works, and not by faith only.*" —James 2:24

Faith and works go hand in hand. How can we ensure that we have not received the grace of God in vain (2 Cor. 6:1)?

13.) Romans 8:16 (NLT) says *"For his Holy Spirit speaks to us deep in our hearts and tells us that we are God's children."* The Holy Spirit witnesses to our hearts that we are indeed children of God. But this can be very subjective—from our own point of view it is a reality—but it may not be true from an objective point of view. And so God gives us another way to know if we really do know the Lord.

Besides the inner witness of the Holy Spirit, what is the other way the New Testament shows us that we can know we are saved?

14.) What is the balance here? Everyone who sins certainly is not disqualified from heaven. Write how "practicing sin" differs from the person who is genuinely struggling, crying out to God for deliverance from sin(s).

15.) A heavenly assignment
   "For the grace of God that brings salvation has appeared to all men. It teaches us to say 'No' to ungodliness and worldly passions, and to live self-controlled, upright and godly lives in this present age, while we wait for the blessed hope— the glorious appearing of our great God and Savior, Jesus Christ, who gave himself for us to redeem us from all wickedness and to purify for himself a people that are his very own, eager to do what is good. These, then, are the things you should teach. Encourage and rebuke with all authority. Do not let anyone despise you. —Titus 2:11-15, NIV

For this last part of today's session, be really creative. Imagine you are a pastor, Bible teacher, or a powerful preacher. You are about to stand in front of thousands of people, and there is a satellite uplink broadcasting your message to millions more around the entire planet! **The Lord Himself has told you to preach a classic three-point sermon using the text of Titus 2:11-15.** You are to use 500 words or less. Here is what God has assigned you to minister on:

- What does it truly mean to be saved
- How your listeners can be saved
- How the Holy Spirit will help them to live a blessed and joyful life as God intends, bearing fruit and obeying God's Word

What will you say as the world watches? How will you say it? Choose your words carefully and prayerfully, and have a blast as you write your "sermon to save the world."

A HEART ABLAZE, IGNITING A PASSION FOR GOD

Mission Nine

2 Peter 3:14 (KJV) says, *"Wherefore, beloved, seeing that ye look for such things, be diligent that ye may be found of him in peace, without spot, and blameless."*

MISSION: PREPARING FOR HIS COMING IN GLORY

1.) The gospel is great news! God has given you the grace that empowers you to change. He transforms your life as you leave behind old ways and move forward to knowing Jesus intimately. You can live a new life of true joy, purity, and separation from the sinfulness of the world!

It seems though that people frequently become inspired to change, getting emotionally hyped up or impressed upon by some experience, and then make declarations of positive change, repentance, and an adjusted lifestyle—only to find a short time later, they are back to the same old ways.

How does trying to live holy and pure in your own strength compare with living in the grace of God?

TRANSFORMED WITHIN

2.) *"For it is God who works in you both to will and to do for His good pleasure."* —Philippians 2:13

The gift that keeps on giving?

TV and magazine ads declare, "It's the gift that keeps on giving!" Their products will keep you perpetually happy, they say. Of course, the reality is quite different. But God's grace is the one thing that advertisers should shout about. It truly is a gift that keeps on giving. As God gives grace in your life, you will find He gives more IN ADDITION to what He already has given. And then He gives more on top of that. It is a never-ending gift from an infinite source: God Himself!

"But He gives us more and more grace (power of the Holy Spirit, to meet this evil tendency and all others fully). That is why He says, God sets Himself against the proud and haughty, but gives grace [continually] to the lowly (those who are humble enough to receive it)." —James 4:6, AMP

Besides the power to overcome sinful lifestyles, another of God's great grace gifts is the power to grow in His Word. As you gain any light into the Scriptures, you will notice that more light is given to build on what you have already received. Whenever something gets clarified that you once misunderstood, then other scriptures open up. It is a continual feast of exciting revelation. Like being on a special quest or mission, you find more and more clues and insight into the character of Jesus. Here is an example from the life of a new believer. They come to realize they need help in life. They then learn of the Savior. They then discover the Bible is His message to them. Then they begin reading and progressively move from faith to faith and glory to glory as God builds on each truth leading to the next.

Behold God at work in YOU! Think back and make a list—**in sequence**—of three or four things you have learned progressively, in succession, on your mission. What discovery of truth led you to the next, and then that opened the door of understanding to another? Record here how God has given you a nugget of grace and light, leading to another nugget, then more grace and light, and more, and so on...

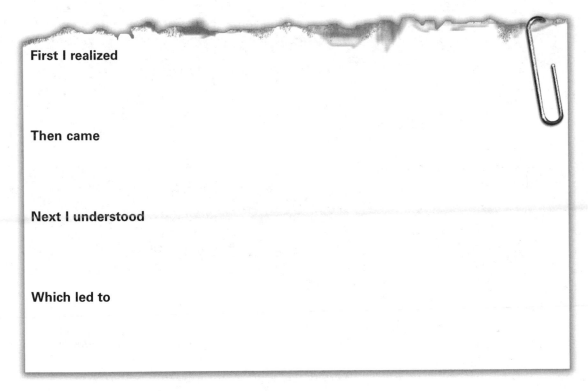

First I realized

Then came

Next I understood

Which led to

3.) *"Strive to live in peace with everybody and pursue that consecration and holiness without which no one will [ever] see the Lord."* —Hebrews 12:14, AMP

In what ways has *A Heart Ablaze* caused you to want to **pursue** consecration—setting yourself apart for the Lord—and holiness?

4.) *"Exercise foresight and be on the watch to look [after one another], to see that no one falls back from and fails to secure God's grace (His unmerited favor and spiritual blessing)...."* —Hebrews 12:15, AMP

"...looking carefully lest anyone fall short of the grace of God..." —Hebrews 12:15

As a believer you are justified in Christ, saved from your sins by grace. But Hebrews

12:14–15 affirms that without *holiness* no one will see the Lord. What is going on here? How do justification, grace, and holiness come together as God's truth for salvation?

5.) *Lifestyle* is a repeated theme of *A Heart Ablaze.* Why do you think this is such an important topic?

6.) Lifestyle *check*
Dig deep. The following provocative questions beg a thoughtful response. Picture Jesus sitting in fellowship with you as you and He work together on your answers:
God is very concerned with your outward lifestyle *and* your inward worship. Why?

How is your lifestyle an accurate reflection of your relationship with the Lord?

Is God more pleased with your public worship or your private times with Him? Is the answer one or the other, or could it be both?

7.)

in·sid·i·ous (ĭn-sĭd-sʹē-əs) *adj.,* **1.** working or spreading harmfully in a subtle or stealthy manner: *insidious rumors; an insidious disease.* **2.** intended to entrap; treacherous: *insidious misinformation.* **3.** beguiling but harmful; alluring: *insidious pleasures.*[9]

Read these very first three words of 2 Timothy 3:1 (AMP).
"But understand this..."

Paul in essence was saying, "Listen up!" "Make sure you get this." "Pay attention!" He goes on to say:

"...that in the last days will come (set in) perilous times of great stress and trouble [hard to deal with and hard to bear]. For people will be lovers of self and [utterly] self-centered, lovers of money and aroused by an inordinate [greedy] desire for wealth, proud and arrogant and contemptuous boasters. They will be abusive (blasphemous, scoffing), disobedient to parents, ungrateful, unholy and profane. [They will be] without natural [human] affection (callous and inhuman), relentless (admitting of no truce or appeasement); [they will be] slanderers (false accusers, troublemakers), intemperate and loose in morals and conduct, uncontrolled and fierce, haters of good. [They will be] treacherous [betrayers], rash, [and] inflated with self-conceit. [They will be] lovers of sensual pleasures and vain amusements more than and rather than lovers of God." —2 Timothy 3:1-4, AMP

Relativism attempts to rule

A Heart Ablaze speaks to issues that may be difficult to face. *Yet that is the very reason this message is so critical for us today.* The toughest issue we may face today is not the overt, "black-and-white" nature of sin in our culture and society. **In fact, it seems there is little that is black and white. It is far more likely that the danger is in the subtle "gray" areas that are so insidious.** How easy it is to be infected with the compromise that spreads so powerfully even among believers!

- **Instead of truth or rational thought, right and wrong are interpreted in light of what is good for self.**
- **We become a people who almost lightheartedly *adjust truth and all standards* to accommodate our own pleasure, our own pursuits, and self-gratification.**
- **We justify our lifestyle of self by declaring, "It's OK as long as it doesn't hurt anyone else."**
- **In more extreme cases, we don't even *care* if it harms others.**

This relativism is a sobering reality of life today! There are so many voices! Politics, business, religion, the seemingly all-powerful media, the arts, the role of the church, the definition of family, career goals—are there no clear cut answers as to what IS right and what is wrong and how we are to live our lives?

Be a news reporter for a few minutes. You are the religion editor of a large metropolitan newspaper. Write a 100-200 word article about this challenge and how you see the Word of God as the answer to today's relativistic society.

8.) You've just received word from the publisher that your article was well received. People want to know more. You are to write another article about intimacy with Jesus as the answer to people's burning desire for fulfillment and gratification in life.

9.) What are some ways you see so called "gray areas" causing compromise today?

10.) Here is an important Bible verse about determining who truly is—as opposed to those who only claim to be—a believer. It is also about the power of grace and its ability to influence how we conduct our own lives. What is the apostle Paul trying to get his protégé, Pastor Timothy, and the church to understand in 2 Timothy 3:5 (AMP)?

*For [although] they hold a form of piety (true religion), they deny and reject and are strangers to the power of it [**their conduct belies the genuineness of their profession**]"* *(emphasis added).*

11.) How does Western culture—which is generally rich in wealth and personal freedom—warp the Christian worldview in comparison with other nations and cultures of the world?

12.) Jesus is a faithful and true witness. He never flatters or panders to us. He will always tell us the truth for our good whether we like it or not.

"And to the angel (messenger) of the assembly (church) in Laodicea write: These are the words of the Amen, the trusty and faithful and true Witness, the Origin and Beginning and Author of God's creation: I know your [record of] works and what you are doing; you are neither cold nor hot. Would that you were cold or hot! So, because you are lukewarm and neither cold nor hot, I will spew you out of My mouth!" —Revelation 3:14-16, AMP

Notice that Jesus says He knows our *works*, not our intentions or the feelings in our hearts. Knowing that Christ is always observing our works can be a daunting concept, even a bit scary. Yet it is without question that God is ever present and all-powerful, beholding even the sparrow, the ant, and the flowers of the field. How much more must He measure the conduct of His very own children!

Here God announces that He will spew the lukewarm out of His mouth. Of course no one wants that. The fear of the Lord is the beginning of wisdom. If you are a believer, *you will live differently than the world. You will come to the realization that Jesus is within you— not only to help you and bless you, but He is observing you as well!*

Write a prayer to the Lord, describing conversationally how this makes you feel:
Awestruck, humbled, cautious, fearful, joyful, hopeful? Let it all out in a prayer that tells God exactly how you feel. AND tell Him how you are seeking Him and depending on His grace to empower you to please Him as both intimate friend and God of the universe!

13.) *"For you say, I am rich; I have prospered and grown wealthy, and I am in need of nothing; and you do not realize and understand that you are wretched, pitiable, poor, blind, and naked. Therefore I counsel you to purchase from Me gold refined and tested by fire, that you may be [truly] wealthy, and white clothes to clothe you and to keep the shame of your nudity from being seen, and salve to put on your eyes, that you may see."* —Revelation 3:17–18, AMP

Why are the lost sheep within the ranks of the "church" harder to reach than those who are not religious?

14.)   Many believe they will be received into heaven, but they will not. This is a chilling thought. Look at what the Lord says about this.

"Those whom I [dearly and tenderly] love, I tell their faults and convict and convince and reprove and chasten [I discipline and instruct them]. So be enthusiastic and in earnest and burning with zeal and repent [changing your mind and attitude]."
—Revelation 3:19, AMP

What is a key—revealed in this passage—to how we may ensure we will be received into heaven, with the Lord in eternity?

15.)   *"But the day of the Lord will come as a thief in the night; in the which the heavens shall pass away with a great noise, and the elements shall melt with fervent heat, the earth also and the works that are therein shall be burned up. Seeing then that these things shall be dissolved, what manner of persons ought ye to be in all holy conversation and godliness, looking for and hasting unto the coming of the day of God, wherein the heavens being on fire shall be dissolved, and the elements shall melt with fervent heat? Nevertheless we, according to his promise, look for new heavens and a new earth, wherein dwelleth righteousness. Wherefore, beloved, seeing that ye look for such things, be diligent that ye may be found of him in peace, without spot, and blameless."*
—2 Peter 3:10-14, KJV

It is so good of God to have clearly laid out His desires for us. Jesus wants our whole heart and life, not just some or even most. We are likened to a bride who is to be pure for her groom. Look at the verses above (2 Pet. 3:10-14). We are plainly told in easily understood language what type of people we are to be. It doesn't get any simpler than that, praise God!

It is so beautiful and wondrous! The last portion of the verse calls us "beloved" and tells us to look after these things and look forward to Jesus returning. **Write how you envision a lifestyle that would prove that the person living it is looking to the coming of Jesus for His spotless bride.**

A HEART ABLAZE, IGNITING A PASSION FOR GOD

Mission Ten

Revelation 3:18 in the NIV says, *"I counsel you to buy from me gold refined in the fire, so that you can become rich; and white clothes to wear, so that you can cover your shameful nakedness; and salve to put on your eyes, so that you can see."*

MISSION: GOLD, WHITE GARMENTS AND EYE SALVE

1.) John the Baptist was sent by God to the "lost sheep of the house of Israel." What does that mean?

What does that have to do with today's church?

"When you come out of the meeting of a prophet, a true prophet, whether man or woman, you will want to seek God more than you have wanted to seek Him before, and you will sense a knowing of Him more than you have ever sensed you've known Him.

"A false prophet, however, will draw you to his gift. When you leave the meeting of a true prophet you want to go pray, but when you leave the meeting of a false prophet, you want to go back and get another word. So, false prophets will use their giftings to attract you and draw you to themselves rather than to the heart of God."

—John Bevere

2.) Throughout all of Scripture, what is the basic message of God's prophets?

Heavenly mission: Be a Detective, find the meaning in scriptures!

2 Timothy 2:15 says, *"Study to shew thyself approved unto God, a workman that needeth not to be ashamed, rightly dividing the word of truth"* (KJV). **It's a fact, study = empowerment and transformation!**

Here are three words or terms you may encounter when you hear sermons or study the Bible. *Biblical exegesis* is a term used to describe an extensive and critical interpretation of the Bible. It means to draw the meaning out of the portion of scripture. The point of good, sound, biblical exegesis is to view the text objectively. Its opposite would be *eisegesis*, which is subjective and means to read one's own interpretation into the text. As Christians we must take care not to impose or imagine our own interpretations into Scripture, but to read the Bible in context and let the Holy Spirit illuminate the passages.

You may also come across *hermeneutics* (think of this as interpreting and under-standing) and *exposition,* or *expository preaching*, which is related to explaining the Bible.

Bible study can take some time, but it is the most rewarding of efforts! Small portions—even a few minutes daily—will yield rich eternal and practical rewards. And you don't have to be a Bible scholar to follow good principles of understand-ing the Word of God. Some passages are more easily understood, plain to nearly everyone, and easily applied. Others are not so simple.

Here is a quick three-point method everyone can use to study the Bible:
1. **Truth**: Ask yourself what the passage is really saying. When, where, why, and to whom was it written? Break it down a bit: What is the book as a whole about, then the chapter, then single words or phrases?
2. **Explanation**: Once you have determined what it is truly communicating, you can begin to explain the text. What is its main point? What did it mean to the original audience and to today's reader? What are the other passages that are similar or comparable to it? Are there principles it teaches?
3. **Application**: Look back at your explanation. How did the passage apply to the original audience, and how can you apply these things today? Are there meaningful differences? What action is the passage leading you to take? How is it speaking to your lifestyle?

Practical Mission: How exciting! *Now, let's do it!* **Read the two passages below and utilize portions of the three-point method to give your study both accuracy and personal meaning.** Additionally, of course, you may use the teaching in this session of *A Heart Ablaze* to help you as well.

"*Because you say, 'I am rich, have become wealthy, and have need of nothing'—and do not know that you are wretched, miserable, poor, blind, and naked—I counsel you to buy from Me gold refined in the fire, that you may be rich; and white garments, that you may be clothed, that the shame of your nakedness may not be revealed; and anoint your eyes with eye salve, that you may see. As many as I love, I rebuke and chasten. Therefore be zealous and repent. Behold, I stand at the door and knock. If anyone hears My voice and opens the door, I will come in to him and dine with him, and he with Me. To him who overcomes I will grant to sit with Me on My throne, as I also overcame and sat down with My Father on His throne. He who has an ear, let him hear what the Spirit says to the churches." —Revelation 3:17-22*

"*'Behold, I send My messenger,*
And he will prepare the way before Me.
And the Lord, whom you seek,
Will suddenly come to His temple,
Even the Messenger of the covenant,
In whom you delight.
Behold, He is coming,'
Says the LORD of hosts.
'But who can endure the day of His coming?
And who can stand when He appears?
For He is like a refiner's fire
And like launderers' soap.
He will sit as a refiner and a purifier of silver;
He will purify the sons of Levi,
And purge them as gold and silver,
That they may offer to the LORD
An offering in righteousness.'" —Malachi 3:1-3

3.) What is the central *truth* contained in these passages? What are they really saying?

4.) Give your *explanation* of the passages (the main point[s], how it compares with others, any principles, etc.):

5.) Now what is the personal *application*? How can you apply these truths in your life?

6.) **The Furnace of Affliction**

Holiness is not a work of your flesh but of God's grace. As you seek the Lord, God will at times allow a refining process in your life as He brings impurities to the surface. These are things that can be unattractive and disturbing as they are revealed, even surprising us as we see our hearts and works of our flesh exposed to God's light and fire.

When we go through the refining process, what happens if we...
choose to become blind to...
continually resist...
blame circumstances for...
blame other people for...
...the things God is revealing in us?

7.) *"And those who are Christ's have crucified the flesh with its passions and desires."*
—Galatians 5:24
The trials of your life can cause the impurities in your life to surface. How should you respond when this happens?

8.)   Much like a ladle scooping impurities from the surface of refined molten metals, what is the result of God's refining fires when we respond properly?

Bring it all **together!**

A Heart Ablaze is not intended to be a lightweight encounter to ease our Christian conscience or have a wealthy lifestyle. **This is your personal mission to know God intimately and be transformed by Him.**

It is so important that we absorb truth and make it real in our minds, hearts, and bodies—our very lifestyle! Remember our verse in 2 Timothy about study. It said "*a workman,*" meaning that God expects some real effort on our part so we can understand and apply these truths. Let's do exactly that. Read the following passages thoroughly:

"Nevertheless the solid foundation of God stands, having this seal: 'The Lord knows those who are His,' and, 'Let everyone who names the name of Christ depart from iniquity.' But in a great house there are not only vessels of gold and silver, but also of wood and clay, some for honor and some for dishonor. Therefore if anyone cleanses himself from the latter, he will be a vessel for honor, sanctified and useful for the Master, prepared for every good work. Flee also youthful lusts; but pursue righteousness, faith, love, peace with those who call on the Lord out of a pure heart." —2 Timothy 2:19 -22

"But God's truth stands firm like a foundation stone with this inscription: 'The Lord knows those who are his,' and 'Those who claim they belong to the Lord must turn away from all wickedness.'
In a wealthy home some utensils are made of gold and silver, and some are made of wood and clay. The expensive utensils are used for special occasions, and the cheap ones are for everyday use. If you keep yourself pure, you will be a utensil God can use for his purpose. Your life will be clean, and you will be ready for the Master to use you for every good work. Run from anything that stimulates youthful lust. Follow anything that makes you want to do right. Pursue faith and love and peace, and enjoy the companionship of those who call on the Lord with pure hearts." —2 Timothy 2:19-22, NLT

"But put on the Lord Jesus Christ, and make no provision for the flesh, to fulfill its lusts."
—Romans 13:14

*"Let us be glad and rejoice and give Him glory, for the marriage of the Lamb has come, and His wife has **made herself** ready."* —Revelation 19:7, emphasis added

"I will greatly rejoice in the LORD, my soul shall be joyful in my God; for he hath clothed me with the garments of salvation, he hath covered me with the robe of righteousness, as a bridegroom decketh himself with ornaments, and as a bride adorneth herself with her jewels." —Isaiah 61:10, KJV

- Wood is symbolic of our flesh.
- Gold is symbolic of a lifestyle that glorifies God.
- Garments are a type of righteousness.
- Eye salve speaks of a clear perception of the character of God.
- Personal responsibility is a given.

There is a lot of truth in these few verses. You've been given a good start here. **Use your three-point Bible study method** and the renewed mind and heart God has given you. Take 5 or 10 minutes of quiet. Remember what you have learned so far in the *A Heart Ablaze* curriculum. **Now, write in #9, 10, and 11 how these passages are an excellent summary of the *A Heart Ablaze* message and its meaning in your life:**

9.)　Truth. What is the *central set of truths* contained in these verses?

10.)　Explanation. What do these truths actually *mean*?

11.)　Application. How do these truths apply to *YOU*?

12.)　Israel was repeatedly corrected for her inaccurate perceptions of God. The people simply didn't know who God was or what He really wanted and expected from them. But there are notable exceptions to this. Moses, Joshua, Caleb, David, Abraham, Hannah, Esther, and many others in the Old and New Testaments rightly discerned God. They

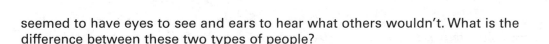
seemed to have eyes to see and ears to hear what others wouldn't. What is the difference between these two types of people?

13.) Jeremiah 29:11 reads, *"'For I know the plans I have for you,' declares the Lord, 'plans to prosper you and not to harm you, plans to give you hope and a future.'"* NIV

We all have dreams and desires, hopes and ambitions. You've come far enough along now to think about yours in light of all you've learned so far. What are they? How has God shaped them since you've begun this study? If you haven't yet put your future plans and dreams under the scrutiny of God's Word, now is a good time to do it.

Complete one of the following:

How has God shaped or even changed your dreams and desires for the future since you've begun this study?

~OR~

If you've not yet thought about it and haven't yet submitted your future plans and dreams to your newfound light from *A Heart Ablaze*, do it now and record some of your thoughts here:

14.) *"One of their religion scholars spoke for them, posing a question they hoped would show him up: 'Teacher, which command in God's Law is the most important?' Jesus said, '"Love the Lord your God with all your passion and prayer and intelligence." This is the most important, the first on any list. But there is a second to set alongside it: "Love* *others as well as you love yourself." These two commands are pegs; everything in God's Law and the Prophets hangs from them.'"* —Matthew 22:35-40, The Message

"Then one of them, a lawyer, asked Him a question, testing Him, and saying, 'Teacher, which is the great commandment in the law?' Jesus said to him, '"You shall love the LORD *your God with all your heart, with all your soul, and with all your mind." This is the first and great commandment. And the second is like it: "You shall love your neighbor as yourself." On these two commandments hang all the Law and the Prophets.'"* —Matthew 22:35-40

- Diligent studying to know His ways...
- Fellowshiping with God – spending time with Him in prayer, praise, and worship...
- These are priority one!

But there is another command alongside this. If passionate study and prayer make up one part of loving God, the other would be fellowship with His saints and reaching out to unbelievers.

How do you see these going hand in hand with one another as the fulfillment of God's desire for us?

15.) Amazing news you'll love to hear!

One ditch:
Are we to fulfill God's commandments and please Him through a lifetime of frustration and impossible fleshly works, ever striving to be perfect keeping the law in and of ourselves?

The other ditch:
Or do we fall into the opposite side of the ditch and throw in the towel, living a life of sin and lasciviousness, never even trying to live a godly lifestyle?

The blessed but narrow highway to heaven:
We need not respond in either of those ways. **Matthew 25:23 and Matthew 6:33 offer the simple, humble answers we seek:**

*"His lord said to him, 'Well done, good and faithful servant; **you have been faithful over a few things, I will make you ruler over many things**. Enter into the joy of your lord.'"* Matthew 25:23, emphasis added

"But seek first the kingdom of God and His righteousness, and all these things shall be added to you." —Matthew 6:33

It is so simple! God's way for us is to grow in grace. His plan for us is to mature from faith to faith and glory to glory. **By being faithful in the things God shows us one at a time, little by little, we soon can move mountains!**

 Set your Heart Ablaze! You've learned secrets of study. Now learn secrets of prayer!

Journal here a prayer of grace, glory, and faith. Pour out your heart to God and record it below.

Here is a guideline for prayer:
- Seek His refining fire, His white garments, and His eyes to see.
- Ask Him to empower you through the Holy Spirit and His Word to take things ONE STEP AT A TIME in your life, pacing yourself in His strength as you serve Him.
- Ask God to show you how to love Him with all of your mind, heart, and strength, and your neighbor as yourself.
- **Praying the actual scriptures is one of the most powerful things you can ever learn in life.** Recite Matthew 25:23 and Matthew 6:33 and any others you desire, quoting them to God in impassioned faith asking for His blessing and promises in them.

A HEART ABLAZE, IGNITING A PASSION FOR GOD

Mission Eleven

Hebrews 12:25 says. *"See that you do not refuse Him who speaks. For if they did not escape who refused Him who spoke on earth, much more shall we not escape if we turn away from Him who speaks from heaven."*

MISSION: BUILDING GODLY CHARACTER

"Of all the properties which belong to honorable men, not one is so highly prized as that of character." —Henry Clay

Let's have some fun as we go on a fast-paced and richly rewarding Scripture study. Notice that you will be using some of the same simple Bible study techniques you learned in your previous session. You can utilize them for the rest of your life to grow supernaturally in God's Word.

chasten (chā´sən), *v.t.* to correct or discipline

"As many as I love, I rebuke and chasten. Therefore be zealous and repent." —Revelation 3:19

"And you have forgotten the exhortation which speaks to you as to sons:
    'My son, do not despise the chastening of the LORD,
    Nor be discouraged when you are rebuked by Him;
    For whom the LORD loves He chastens,
    And scourges every son whom He receives.'
If you endure chastening, God deals with you as with sons; for what son is there whom a father does not chasten?" —Hebrews 12:5-7

Verse 6 of Hebrews 12 uses the word *scourge* (meaning "to whip") and speaks of endurance as well. God certainly doesn't scourge us with whips, but His correction can seem severe, requiring humility and endurance. Like a loving parent, God will correct and protect His children, shaping our character, ensuring our healthy growth. We are to be thankful for it. It shows we are His very own children and He is training us!

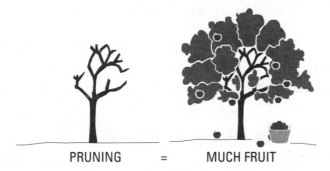

PRUNING   =   MUCH FRUIT

Pruning is another way of understanding God's chastening. Look at the words of the Master, Jesus:

"I am the true vine, and my Father is the gardener. He cuts off every branch that doesn't produce fruit, and he prunes the branches that do bear fruit so they will produce even more. You have already been pruned for greater fruitfulness by the message I have given you. Remain in me, and I will remain in you. For a branch cannot produce fruit if it is severed from the vine, and you cannot be fruitful apart from me. Yes, I am the vine; you are the branches. Those who remain in me, and I in them, will produce much fruit. For apart from me you can do nothing." —John 15:1-5, NLT

God's chastening has to do with our character, and our character will determine the fruit our life produces. God seeks to mold us, bless us, and help us be conformed to His glorious image. He also expects us to bear good and abundant fruit.

1.) Along with the exhortation to endure in Hebrews 12, we are encouraged to "remain" in the Lord in John 15. God is forewarning us, sending us a message that is clear. These words indicate that chastening won't be pleasant and will require some stamina and perseverance. Another way of putting it could be: "It takes some guts—real heart—and strong faith to see this Christian walk through to the end."

You put it into your own words now. Read and keep in mind the above verses from Revelation, Hebrews, and John. Write a few sentences about what it takes to remain, to endure, and to persevere as a believer:

2.) *"Now no chastening seems to be joyful for the present, but painful; nevertheless, afterward it yields the peaceable fruit of righteousness to those who have been trained by it." —* Hebrews 12:11

To yield the best results, a gardener has to make some tough calls and cut back lots of seemingly good branches on a fruit tree. It can be a painstaking process, and at the end there is a pile of leaves, sticks, and branches and a tree that now looks pretty bare and maybe even ugly. At times, the more aggressive the cutting back, the more benefit there will be to the tree!

Onlookers who don't understand the process ask, "Why? Why did you cut and ruin that perfectly good tree?" But next season, all is very well as the old limbs are beautifully replaced with new growth and stronger, healthier branches as the fruit produced by the tree substantially increases in quality and number!

Scripture is wonderfully plain. God's shaping of our lives can be a real challenge. But John 15:5 gives us the key to our staying power. How are we able to endure the often painful process of God's pruning?

3.) Revelation 3 says God corrects and disciplines those whom He loves. What do discipline and correction have to do with love?

4.) Interestingly, John 15:1-5 twice speaks of our remaining in the Lord and His remaining in us, indicating a level of cooperation and expectation. God expects us to do our part, and He promises He will do His. Explain your role of "remaining in the Lord" during times of pruning and chastening.

5.) Isaiah 26:16 says, *"LORD, in trouble they have visited You, they poured out a prayer when Your chastening was upon them."*
In this chapter of Isaiah the people of God have been enduring great trouble, and they consequently go to God in prayer. There are many things that can be learned from reading Isaiah 26. But we will look at two that have bearing on our study. Both are seen here in verse 16.

First, it says "in trouble they have visited You." This is loaded with implications! God does not seek visitation; He desires habitation. Often our tendency is to only seek closeness with the Lord when times are hard. While it is true that these situations can draw us close to Jesus, it is certainly not God's best that we only seek Him in times of trouble.

God's first way of correcting us is through His Word. He gives us the Word so we can choose to live a life of blessed obedience and fellowship with Him. But often we are stubborn or rebellious and won't respond to this. So God's next avenue of discipline in our lives is often affliction (Ps. 119:67, 75; I Cor. 11:30-32). God wants our instant obedience and our heart of humility to obey His Word now, instead of resisting Him and His ways.

How can you adjust your heart and lifestyle **from** one of only seeking God when you need Him **to** a life of greater blessing—a life empowered by God's fellowship, ablaze with and for God's heart **at all times**?

6.) The other truth to grasp in Isaiah 26:16 is taken from the second portion of the scripture: *"They poured out a prayer when Your chastening was upon them."*
What is revealed here about how we can and must respond to God's correction and pruning?

7.) Much of God's dealing in our life will be correction. Wise children will ultimately welcome discipline and the blessings that it brings to their lives. Proverbs 12:15 declares that only fools despise or resist correction, while wise men and women heed God's counsel.

*"The way of a fool is right in his own eyes,
But he who heeds counsel is wise."*

A fool is one who sees his _____ thoughts and life as the measure of

wisdom. A fool is one who is _____.

TRANSFORMED WITHIN

"For it is God who works in you both to will and to do for His good pleasure."
—Philippians 2:13

Repentance does not have to be emotional; it just needs to be real. It means you truly let go of *your* ways, *your* wisdom, and *your* worldly ideas of what is truth and instead embrace God's ways. Going through the pain or motions of correction but not repenting is of no real value. You must desire to change from where you presently are to God's glorious nature.

In previous sessions you have identified some challenges or obstacles presently in your life that are hindering you from being the person God wants you to be. Think once again about these areas.

8.) Record how God is continuing to speak to you and work in you *in repentance and lifestyle* as you go on your personal mission through *A Heart Ablaze*.

9.) Think about how you have personally seen the Lord working throughout your own life and the lives of others as He rebukes, disciplines, corrects, and prunes. Write down some examples from *the past.*

10.) As you seek Him, God IS working in you for good things! How have you seen the rewards, positive growth, and more abundant fruit of those times in the past (#9) when God was working?

11.) "*If God gives such attention to the appearance of wildflowers—most of which are never even seen—don't you think he'll attend to you, take pride in you, do his best for you? What I'm trying to do here is to get you to relax, to not be so preoccupied with getting, so you can respond to God's giving. People who don't know God and the way He works fuss over these things, but you know both God and how He works. Steep your life in God-reality, God-initiative, God-provisions. Don't worry about missing out. You'll find all your everyday human concerns will be met.*" —Matthew 6:30-33, The Message

Most of us can see where God has worked in the past in our lives. Holiness, righteousness, peace, wisdom, strength, joy, healing, and prosperity are some of the things God blesses us with as we seek first His kingdom, His heart.

How will your relationship and intimacy with God deepen as you are changed from glory to glory forsaking the things of this world, repenting, serving, and putting Him first instead?

The unfolding **drama**

12.) *"See that you do not refuse Him who speaks."* —Hebrews 12:25
We've talked about it in earlier sessions. We live in a world that tends very strongly to be relativistic, adjusting truth to our desires instead of following God's standards. This verse is a strong admonition from the writer of Hebrews. It is God's voice and will being made known to the reader. Why is it so emphatic, so important? The Message puts it this way: *"So don't turn a deaf ear to these gracious words."*

Remember what you've learned about correction. Do you think this verse implies any consequences for those who do refuse to take heed?

REACHING OUT

13.) *"Thus, by their fruit you will recognize them. Not everyone who says to me, 'Lord, Lord,' will enter the kingdom of heaven, but only he who does the will of my Father who is in heaven."*
—Matthew 7:20–21, NIV

"Nothing is more shattering than Bible truth." —Leonard Ravenhill[10]

"In this day of thin theology, gospel peddlers (I hardly dare call them evangelists) have accented free grace until some such teaching has become a disgrace."
—Leonard Ravenhill[11]

In much of today's society it is considered unsophisticated or insensitive to talk about the consequences of one's actions. The Bible and even commonsense truth may be sneered at or derided. **This is a good time to realize that God's Word is not a book of suggestions or good ideas spoken by good men and women.** It is the very Word of the King of kings, the Sovereign Ruler of the universe. Jesus Christ is God, and He made His will known in the Scriptures.

At times the Bible may offend us or our sensibilities. Jesus did so constantly, for good reason; so did his prophets. It was their job to confront as well as bless, for the good of humanity. And so, as you are out in the world, at your job or in school—wherever your life takes you—you will need strength, fortitude, and lots of God's grace to enable you to stand firm in the will of God.

Perhaps one of the most powerful ways we can **reach out** to others is by being a strong, solid witness for Christ in our everyday lives. Simply having the reputation of being someone who actually lives what he professes may be your strongest ally in extending your faith to others. That way when you do speak, you will have their confidence.

How can you do this? What can you do to bolster yourself against caving in to peer pressure, family or friends, and society at large when you are tempted or you feel the heat to deny God's Word?

14.) *"See that you do not refuse Him who speaks. For if they did not escape who refused Him who spoke on earth, much more shall we not escape if we turn away from Him who speaks from heaven."* —Hebrews 12:25
Why is there a greater judgment on us today than what was on the people of Israel when it comes to hearing and obeying God's voice?

15.) *"Whose voice then shook the earth; but now He has promised, saying, 'Yet once more I shake not only the earth, but also heaven.' Now this, 'Yet once more,' indicates the removal of those things that are being shaken, as of things that are made, that the things which cannot be shaken may remain. Therefore, since we are receiving a kingdom which cannot be shaken, let us have grace, by which we may serve God acceptably with reverence and godly fear."* —Hebrews 12:26-28

a. God has promised that He WILL shake not only the things that are eternal but also the things that are not built on a proper foundation. You want to be one that remains, able to endure the shaking. The scripture here gives the key, the answer: What does the verse teach about this? How can you be one that remains?

b. *"For our God is a consuming fire."* —Hebrews 12:29

What a great verse to finish this session with! God the consuming fire is real, alive, and coming again! No one knows the day of His appearing. We must be wise and be ready now and every day.

A Heart Ablaze speaks of fire. You have learned of the refining furnace, of God's appearing in fire at Sinai, and other types of fire in the Scriptures. Why does the writer of Hebrews sum up his thought in this passage with this verse? Could it be to warn us? Or encourage us? Both?

c. Journal here what Jesus—**shown here as God-the-Consuming-Fire**—means to you, **personally**, in your mission of *A Heart Ablaze*.

"What the writer of the New Testament is saying is, 'Listen, you've got grace now, and grace gives you the ability to cleanse yourself in the fear of the Lord, perfecting holiness in the fear of God, right? So, therefore do it, because if they didn't escape who refused the voice of Him who spoke from Sinai, how much more if we refuse Him who speaks from heaven.'"

—John Bevere

A HEART ABLAZE, IGNITING A PASSION FOR GOD

Mission Twelve

Revelation 3:19 says, *"As many as I love, I rebuke and chasten.
Therefore be zealous and repent."*

MISSION: HOLY FIRE WITHIN

"Pride keeps us from His chastening, thus we forfeit the benefit of the work of His holiness. If we humble ourselves and accept His chastening, we are enabled to hear His voice with greater accuracy and see with greater clarity."

—John Bevere

That statement is loaded with God's message to us! Let's break it down as we go through this last session of *A Heart Ablaze.*

*"When pride comes, then comes shame;
But with the humble is wisdom."* —Proverbs 11:2

God corrects His children. If you receive no chastening, then you're not His child. But even if God is using His Word or circumstances to discipline us, our pride can undermine God's working in us.
Let's examine the contrast of those who humbly receive God's dealings versus those who react in pride.

1.) A Story of Humility or Pride
Imagine an event where God has repeatedly brought His Word to someone. Through

Bible study, sermons at church, even through friends and family this individual has received numerous words from the Lord about how Scripture and God's ways apply to his current lifestyle or situation:

Joe is seeing Angie. Joe always champions how he is a dedicated believer, a strong Christian. He met Angie at the beach. He was going to relax, swim, and reflect while reading a book about prayer. Angie, tall, tanned and attractive, literally bumped into Joe at the snack counter. She was there with a group of friends buying a few more beers to take back to their beach party. She and Joe laughed about their collision and seemed to really hit it off, and the next thing he knew, Joe had her phone number and was dating her. Angie is fun and always seems carefree. She goes to the beach nearly every day, partying with friends and acquaintances, often spending the night wherever she finds herself. She is moving out of her previous boyfriend's condominium and is hoping to find a new place soon. She says she used to have a Christian friend that told her about being "born again." Angie tells Joe she is "open to God" and really "has a lot of faith." Once she "experiences more of life," she will "settle down with a family and decide what religion will best suit [her] lifestyle."

Joe feels a bit uneasy hanging out with Angie and her friends, and lately even his prayers seem to suggest that he is confused about their relationship. Joe's pastor has recently been preaching a series on relationships and how believers are not to be unequally joined together with nonbelievers. Witnessing is one thing, he says, but dating and marriage are something else entirely. His sermons have also shown how believers can be in the world but not of it.

Joe's family has repeatedly asked him how he sees Angie fitting in with God's teachings and his professed faith. Joe's friends have expressed concern that he is falling for someone who simply does not hold to his beliefs and lifestyle. Joe's long-time best friend Cliff works construction with Joe every day and has asked Joe why he sees signs of compromise in Joe's life lately.

God seems to be going to great lengths to get a message through to Joe. Joe claims to be one who hears and follows God's words.

What do you think God is trying to tell Joe?

Why do you think Joe seems to be having difficulty hearing what God is saying?

How *should* Joe respond to these things? Proverbs 11:2 says, "*With the humble is wisdom.*" Write a description of what Joe should do—what action he must take—in this situation if he is to humbly respond to God's correction.

Write a description of how Joe might react in pride or self-will to God's correction, as opposed to humility.

Let's take a look into the future. Proverbs 11:2 declares, "*When pride comes, then comes shame.*" If Joe doesn't respond humbly to God's leading through his church, family, and friends, he will probably end up experiencing the next level of God's chastening. This may be affliction brought on by Joe's decisions but allowed by God.

If Joe continues to be involved with Angie, what might Joe's future look like? Think in terms of how God uses circumstances and the consequences of our actions to chasten us and bring us to repentance.

2.) *"But we all, with unveiled face, beholding as in a mirror the glory of the Lord, are being transformed into the same image from glory to glory, just as by the Spirit of the Lord."* —2 Corinthians 3:18.

There is a great benefit to responding properly to God's correction. Obedience and humility tend to build exponentially, creating godly momentum in our lives. The more we humbly obey, the more we tend to humbly obey. We gain *clarity* in our life, thoughts, and actions. We go from "glory to glory."

Pride and a stubborn heart, however, create the opposite momentum. We go from deception to more deception as opposed to glory; a downward spiral of self-will, our eyes becoming more and more blinded to any truth at all.

When we accept God's chastening, choosing His way instead of ours, it acts as a purifier to our souls. Crooked paths become straight, mountains are removed, valleys are filled, the smoke clears, and we can see and breathe freely. We hear the voice of the Lord more accurately and see His leadings more clearly.

Describe in your own words how seeking and responding humbly to God's leading and correction **cut through** the worldly fog and confusion that so constantly blur our sensibilities and cloud both our reasoning and perception of God and His will.

3.) *"I will stand my watch*
And set myself on the rampart,
And watch to see what He will say to me,
And what I will answer when I am corrected." —Habakkuk 2:1

"Uzziah was sixteen years old when he became king, and he reigned fifty-two years in Jerusalem. His mother's name was Jecholiah of Jerusalem. And he did what was right in the sight of the Lord, according to all that his father Amaziah had done. He sought God in the days of Zechariah, who had understanding in the visions of God; and as long as he sought the Lord, God made him prosper." —2 Chronicles 26:3-5

We can learn principles all the time, but truly following them is a different story. God's principles are revealed in this verse about King Uzziah and also in the words of the prophet Habakkuk.

Both passages lead to the same set of truths, a path of life we can all follow.
- We must be watchful and mindful of God's leading, correction, and Word.
- Our response to—how we answer—His Word determines our outcome in life now and eternally.
- As long as we seek Him, we will prosper.

Think back to Joe and Angie. Joe isn't the only one God was speaking to. Angie had spiritual leanings, and God had reached out to her in her past.

What about you? Are you like Joe or maybe Angie? Or are you very different from them?

Are you watchful? Have you set yourself to see and hear what God REALLY is saying about you and your lifestyle?
It is one thing to be blessed by God, but as His child, how will you answer when you are corrected?

There are few things as powerful as the written word, especially when it is personal and thoughtful. You read about Joe and Angie; **now write your own life's version—in short story form—of God's dealings with you lately.**

Here is an example to help you get started:

The Lord led _____ (insert YOUR name) to read A Heart Ablaze, *watch the videos, and complete the workbook. _____ (insert YOUR name) is a busy mom and executive, but she chose to make this sacrifice of time and effort because she was realizing lately that she needed more of God in her life. Also, she has been struggling with talking about Jesus to her friends at work and even with her family, and she wants to improve in that area. As she began the series, _____ (insert YOUR name) was filled with excitement but also concern. Could she understand it all? Would she see it through? Would it really make for a more blessed life for her?*

As _____ (insert YOUR name) went through the course, God began speaking to her about _____ in her life. She began to see _____ and _____ ...

You get the idea. Tell **your** story, as though it were going in a book or a magazine article. As serious as it is, try to have some fun with this, and you'll see how your own personal drama is unfolding before your very eyes!

4.)   Second Chronicles 26:5 says, "*He sought God in the days of Zechariah, who had understanding in the visions of God; **and as long as he sought the LORD, God made him prosper**" (emphasis added).

The promise of prosperity here is strongly conditional. Notice too that seeking the Lord Himself is the concept, not seeking the good of the King's country or the success of his ministry. Seeking first the kingdom of God and His righteousness causes all other things to fall into place (Matt. 6:33).

The truth about prosperity

Did you ever realize that prosperity does NOT necessarily mean financial wealth at all? Abraham, David, and others had wealth, but it definitely was not the measure of their prosperity. God gave them wealth for the fulfillment of their calling. John the Baptist was blessed by God in ways few could imagine—yet he suffered a martyr's death, beheaded in seeming humility! Jeremiah the weeping prophet, David hiding in caves, Paul the Apostle—these are among the most prosperous and blessed individuals in history, and yet they lived rough and at times dangerous lives. Hannah and later Elizabeth and Mary didn't live the lifestyles of the rich and famous, but few were more blessed than they!

Jesus Himself—God—humiliated, beaten, alone and crucified; does that look like "prosperity" as so many would define it?

There is nothing wrong with wealth itself. But how do you think God defines "prosperity"?

5.) In your own words, from all you have learned in this series, what does it mean to "seek the Lord and prosper"?

6.) Look back in your own life. Elaborate on some ways in which **you sought God and He then made you to prosper.**

Times of crisis, accidents, injuries, doctors' reports, financial needs, relationships—God is there for those who seek Him. What are some **specific** prayer requests you have made in your life in times of need, and what were the specific answers to your prayers?

7.) How about more generally? Family, friends, your career and home, church, peace and contentment, witnessing, personal fulfillment, etc.; how has God prospered you **as a whole** in your life as you simply seek Him daily, as opposed to "crisis" praying?

8.) Business, ministry, parenting, school, whatever God has called us to He will equip us for and prosper us in as we seek Him. But what happens when we step outside of what God has called us to do?

9.) A riveting story!

Talk about real-life drama! Picture a handsome young man, a son of kings. His father dies, and the youth inherits a kingdom. He becomes a man of great wisdom and spirit. He has influence and favor with God and man. Over fifty years he rules, and his fame spreads. At the height of his reign he tragically and publicly loses it all through a prideful impetuous act, becoming a diseased shell of his former greatness.

This is no fairy tale. King Uzziah began his reign at a very young age, and he grew to great power and wealth as he sought God. Later he was lifted up in pride and arrogance and came to a tragic end. Second Chronicles 26:16-21 gives the epic account:

"But when he was strong his heart was lifted up, to his destruction, for he transgressed against the LORD his God by entering the temple of the LORD to burn incense on the altar of incense. So Azariah the priest went in after him, and with him were eighty priests of the LORD—valiant men. And they withstood King Uzziah, and said to him, 'It is not for you, Uzziah, to burn incense to the LORD, but for the priests, the sons of Aaron, who are consecrated to burn incense. Get out of the sanctuary, for you have trespassed! You shall have no honor from the LORD God.' Then Uzziah became furious; and he had a censer in his hand to burn incense. And while he was angry with the priests, leprosy broke out on his forehead, before the priests in the house of the LORD, beside the incense altar. And Azariah the chief priest and all the priests looked at him, and there, on his forehead, he was leprous; so they thrust him out of that place. Indeed he also hurried to get out, because the LORD had struck him. King Uzziah was a leper until the day of his death. He dwelt in an isolated house, because he was a leper; for he was cut off from the house of the LORD. Then Jotham his son was over the king's house, judging the people of the land."

God is so good to give us so much to learn from in His Word. He gives us all we need to live well and stay on course. Notice this account begins with the fact that Uzziah was strong, not weak when he fell! We typically think of failure coming to the weak, but it is actually true that our strength and prosperity can be more precarious for us in our lives than when we may have had little.

Prosperity can be poison to the soul. Strength can corrupt humble hearts.

We spoke of momentum earlier, and going from faith to faith and glory to glory. As we go from victory to victory, it is very possible that the things of success will cause us to cease the very practices that brought us to success. We may forsake the basics such as prayer, humility, hard work, holiness, and servanthood.

Proverbs 4:23 says, *"Keep and guard your heart with all vigilance and above all that you guard, for out of it flow the springs of life"* (AMP).

How is "keeping and guarding our heart" the key to avoiding the spiritual leprosy and physical calamity that can come from the pride of life?

10.) What does "with all vigilance" imply?

11.)   🔹 **Holy, Holy, Holy** 🔹

"The four living creatures, each having six wings, were full of eyes around and within. And they do not rest day or night, saying: 'Holy, holy, holy, Lord God Almighty, who was and is and is to come!'" —Revelation 4:8

"In the year that King Uzziah died, I saw the Lord sitting on a throne, high and lifted up, and the train of His robe filled the temple. Above it stood seraphim; each one had six wings: with two he covered his face, with two he covered his feet, and with two he flew. And one cried to another and said: 'Holy, holy, holy is the LORD of hosts; the whole earth is full of His glory!' And the posts of the door were shaken by the voice of him who cried out, and the house was filled with smoke. So I said: 'Woe is me, for I am undone! Because I am a man of unclean lips, and I dwell in the midst of a people of unclean lips; for my eyes have seen the King, the LORD of hosts.'" —Isaiah 6:1-5

"These angels were not crying, 'Power, power, power.' Is God powerful? Yes, but that's not what they were crying. They weren't crying, 'Love, love, love.' Is God love? Oh, yeah, the Bible says He is love, but they weren't crying love. They weren't crying, 'Light, light, light.' Is He light? Yeah, He's light. They weren't crying, 'Faithful, faithful, faithful.' Is God faithful? Yeah. But what is the attribute of God that stands above all other attributes? It is His holiness. Because you have to understand, the revelation of His glory is His holiness."

—John Bevere

What importance is there in the fact that these scriptures repeat the word "holy" three times?

12.) Isaiah was a great preacher of righteousness, yet what was his response when he saw the glory of the Lord?

13.) What does the word *undone* mean?
[ ] running joyfully [ ] stricken with sadness [ ] angry [ ] hurt [ ] coming apart at the seams

14.) Eternal Love

"There are three things which are too wonderful for me,
Four which I do not understand:
The way of an eagle in the sky,
The way of a serpent on a rock,
The way of a ship in the middle of the sea,
And the way of a man with a maid." —Proverbs 30:18-19, NAS

The way of a man and a maiden; being in love! For this specific portion of our study we are not speaking in any way of the higher love, the *agape* love that is always pure, faithful, and unconditional—the love that God demonstrated toward us and that we are to demonstrate to others through the sacrifice of Christ upon the cross. (See John 15:13.)

Rather, we speak for the moment of the more emotional, visceral love; the way of a man and a woman when they are "falling in love." What can compare to the electricity, the heightened responses, the rushes of emotion and sheer inexplicable pleasure that accompany it?

History is filled with grand love stories. Hollywood plays to our feelings and makes billions of dollars from productions of stories of love. Whatever the theme, these stories tend to capture our hearts and imaginations. The physiological reactions, the chemical responses, the psychological roller coaster are still great mysteries even to modern science, where our society so often looks for enlightenment.

When in love we feel our lover can do no wrong, all is well in the world, and everything else pales in comparison to being with, holding, and beholding the countenance of our love! The object of our focused attention is all we have body, heart, and soul for, and the cares of life and the world fall into blurred relief as we almost blindly stumble under the spell of our love's delights!

It is too wonderful to know, too bewildering to fathom—this engaged and living response—this miraculous, almost supernatural thing we call love. Read Revelation 4:8:

"The four living creatures, each having six wings, were full of eyes around and within. And they do not rest day or night, saying: 'Holy, holy, holy, Lord God Almighty, who was and is and is to come!'"

Here is an amazing and really exciting truth about the love of God we can learn from the fourth chapter of Revelation.

If these creatures do not rest day or night, how is it they don't get bored or tired with always beholding God and declaring His majesty? Why wouldn't they want to go do some other amazing things around the universe or in heaven? What is it that can hold their attention, allegiance, awe, and hearts endlessly without rest?

The answer is: **They are responding to what they see. The glory of God is so intense, so endlessly awesome and beautiful, they simply do not want to do anything or be anywhere else—***forever***!**

The wondrous and nearly addictive way of love between a man and a woman was given to us in part as a type of our relationship with the King of Kings who is coming for His spotless bride! *And as incredibly good as that can be, it pales in comparison to what we will experience when we behold the Lord in glory! God's love is 100 percent pure, unconditional, and unfathomable. It is the opposite of "love is blind." It is perfect clarity. If the angels are endlessly enraptured with our holy God, how much better will be eternity for God's very own children!*

You have learned so much in this series so far. Are you coming to realize that YOU are the object of His incredible and perfect love? And that you can return His love? God has passionate holy desire for you. He wants a love whose heart is on fire, purified by His love; a bride who serves Him and is prepared for Him. God desires us to have a love full of passion to live the adventure of *His* lifestyle; a love that He will keep inflamed in us throughout eternity! Now that's a GREAT and eternal love story—and it is yours for the following!

What fantastic realities these are! Who knew it could be so good? Journal your thoughts and meditations, using your own words to express your love and adoration, your awe at the realization of God's incredible eternal love story.

Satan our enemy deceived Adam and Eve, perverting the character of God. The world often portrays the holiness of God as a negative—a "downer," something to hold us back, stifle, or ruin our fun. Holiness is perceived as an archaic lifestyle that has been left behind by modern society. But Scripture actually teaches the opposite.

The purity and holiness that emanate from God's throne is the very nature of God Himself. As we have seen in earlier sessions, this is another paradox:

The holiness from which the world runs away is the very thing that offers the fulfillment we so deeply long for.

Like the four creatures in Revelation 4, when we experience God's holiness within our lifestyles, we are sublimely content to remain in His presence! It doesn't get any better than that!

Has God increased your longing for His ways through these sessions? Write down some specific ways God has wooed you to Himself throughout your mission:

> "We are called to burn with the fire of God's glory as Moses, as Isaiah, as Jeremiah, as John and Paul and others, but it will never happen if we do not separate ourselves from the world. That is the focus of this entire message."
>
> —John Bevere

A Heart Ablaze has been a no-holds-barred message confronting things that we may hold dear, blazing new trails, dividing truth from lies, and seeking a no-compromise lifestyle. It is good news to those who seek repentance. God is coming in fire that will bless those who have been purified in the trials of life by God's Word and Spirit. But for those who claim to be God's, yet who live unholy, unscriptural lifestyles, it will consume them like stubble, leaving them in eternity without God.

"'Your words have been harsh against Me,' says the LORD, 'yet you say, "What have we spoken against You?" You have said, "It is useless to serve God; what profit is it that we have kept His ordinance, and that we have walked as mourners before the LORD of hosts? So now we call the proud blessed, for those who do wickedness are raised up; they even tempt God and go free."' Then those who feared the LORD spoke to one another, and the LORD listened and heard them; so a book of remembrance was written before Him for those who fear the LORD and who meditate on His name. 'They shall be Mine,' says the LORD of hosts, 'in the day that I make them My jewels. And I will spare them as a man spares his own son who serves him. Then you shall again discern between the righteous and the wicked, between one who serves God and one who does not serve Him. For behold, the day is coming, burning like an oven, and all the proud, yes, all who do wickedly will be stubble. And the day which is coming shall burn them up,' says the LORD of hosts, 'that will leave them neither root nor branch. But to you who fear My name the Sun of Righteousness shall arise with healing in His wings.'" —Malachi 3:13-4:2

It's easy to serve God and say we live well and godly when things are wonderful. **But it is in the times we are challenged that our true character is revealed. How we handle these determines if we have a heart that is ablaze.**

Honestly, from the depths of your heart, how have **you** responded to the challenges in this message?

TRANSFORMED WITHIN

15.) *"For it is God who works in you both to will and to do for His good pleasure."* —Philippians 2:13

Two last mission details

*"And it came to pass, that, while they communed together and reasoned, Jesus himself drew near, and went with them.... And they said one to another, **Did not our heart burn within us, while he talked with us by the way, and while he opened to us the scriptures?**"* —Luke 24:15, 32, KJV, emphasis added

God is speaking. Your comfort, your power, your fire comes from hearing the voice of God's Word. Fearing God, keeping His commandments, and pursuing holiness sum up this entire message. Now it is time to revisit your Personal Mission Statement for *A Heart Ablaze*.

- Read it thoroughly.
- Now be bold. Feel free to adjust it. Tear it apart, re-structure it, or make just few small changes, whichever is appropriate now that you are completing your mission courses. MAKE IT A STATEMENT that will last a lifetime!

Finally, pour out your heart. Work out all your praises, your objections, your thoughts and concerns, your passion, and your needs and desires. Tell the Lord of your love. As you seek Him now, let Him use your pen like a torch and emblazen this page as the psalmist said:

"My insides got hotter and hotter.
My thoughts boiled over;
I spilled my guts." —Psalm 39:3, The Message

Another version puts it a bit more elegantly:

"I felt a fire burning inside,
and the more I thought,
the more it burned,
until at last I said..." —Psalm 39:3, CEV

Say it, write it now:

"Since, then, you have been raised with Christ, set your hearts on things above, where Christ is seated at the right hand of God. Set your minds on things above, not on earthly things. For you died, and your life is now hidden with Christ in God. When Christ, who is your life, appears, then you also will appear with him in glory. Put to death, therefore, whatever belongs to your earthly nature: sexual immorality, impurity, lust, evil desires and greed, which is idolatry. Because of these, the wrath of God is coming. You used to walk in these ways, in the life you once lived. But now you must rid yourselves of all such things as these: anger, rage, malice, slander, and filthy language from your lips. Do not lie to each other, since you have taken off your old self with its practices and have put on the new self, which is being renewed in knowledge in the image of its Creator."
—**Colossians 3:1-10,** NIV

"May your hearts be ablaze with God's fire! God bless you." —John Bevere

Mission Notes

Mission Notes

Mission Notes

Mission Notes

_____

_____

_____

_____

_____

_____

_____

_____

_____

_____

_____

_____

_____

_____

_____

_____

We hope this *A Heart Ablaze* mission has helped you as you continue
on the *life-long* adventure available to those who make the decision
to live each day in obedience to God.

Giving God glory...

If there is a personal story you would like to share
about how this curriculum has touched you,
we would love to hear from you.
mail@messengerintl.org

OUR NEED FOR A SAVIOR

There are two standards for living; one set by society and one set by God. Our culture may deem you "good" according to its parameters, but what does God think? Scripture tells us every person has fallen short of God's standard of right: "As the Scriptures say: 'There is no one who always does what is right, not even one.'" (Rom. 3:10 NCV) and again, "For all have sinned; all fall short of God's glorious standard." (Rom. 3:23 NLT)

To sin means to miss the mark of God's standard. Man was not created to be a sinner; rather Adam chose this course of his own free will. God placed the first man, Adam, in a beautiful world without sickness, disease, poverty, or natural disasters. There was no fear, hatred, strife, jealousy, and so forth. God called this place Eden, the very garden of God.

Adam chose to disobey God's command and experienced an immediate spiritual death, even though he did not die physically until hundreds of years later. Darkness entered his heart, and this spiritual death differs from physical death because in physical death the body ceases to exist; however, spiritual death is best described as separation from God, the very giver and source of all life.

Sin had entered Adam's makeup, and he fathered children after this nature: "And Adam lived one hundred and thirty years, and begot a son in his own likeness, after his image" (Gen. 5:3).

As a father his offspring were born after his nature and from this point forward each and every human is born into the image of his sin through their parents. Adam gave himself and his descendants over to a new lord, Satan, and with this captivity the natural world followed suit. A cruel lord now had legal claim to God's beloved creation. This is made clear in the following verses: "Then the devil, taking Him [Jesus] up on a high mountain, showed Him all the kingdoms of the world in a moment of time. And the devil said to Him, 'All this authority I will give to you, and their glory; for this has been delivered to me, and I give it to whomever I wish'" (Luke 4:5-6, author's emphasis).

Notice it was delivered to him. When? The answer is in the garden, for God originally gave the dominion of earth to man (see Gen. 1:26-28). Adam lost it all...this included himself and his seed for all generations. Again we read, "The whole world lies under the sway of the wicked one" (1 John 5:19).

Before God sent Adam from the garden, He made a promise. A deliverer would arise and destroy the bondage and captivity mankind had been subjected to.

This deliverer was born four thousand years later to a virgin named Mary. She had to be a virgin, as the father of Jesus was the Holy Spirit who impregnated her. If Jesus had been born to natural parents, He would have been born into the captivity of Adam.

He was Fathered by God and His mother was human. This made Him completely God and completely man. It had to be a son of man, who would purchase our freedom. For this reason Jesus constantly referred to Himself as the "Son of man." Though He was with the Father from the beginning, He stripped Himself of His divine privileges and became a man in order to give Himself as an offering for sin.

When He went to the cross, He took the judgment of our sin on Himself to free us from our bondage. Scripture declares, "He personally carried away our sins in his own body on the cross so we can be dead to sin and live for what is right." (1 Peter 2:24, NLT)

It's amazing: man sinned against God, and yet God (manifest in the flesh) paid the price for man's grave err. We read again, "For God made Christ, who never sinned, to be the offering for our sin, so that we could be made right with God through Christ." (2 Cor. 5:20-21, NLT)

Notice it says we could be made right. We do not receive the freedom which He paid so great a price for until we believe in our hearts that He died for us and was raised from the dead, and receive Him as our Lord; that is when He becomes our personal Savior. As Scripture states, "But to all who believed him and accepted him, he gave the right to become children of God. They are reborn! This is not a physical birth resulting from human passion or plan - this rebirth comes from God." (John 1:12-13, NLT)

When we receive Jesus Christ as our personal Lord and Savior, we die and are spiritually reborn. We die as slaves in the kingdom of Satan and are born as brand new children of God in His kingdom. How does this happen? Simple, when we believe this in our heart all we have to do is confess with our mouth Jesus as our Lord, and we are born again. Scripture affirms this: "For if you confess with your mouth that Jesus is Lord and believe in your heart that God raised him from the dead, you will be saved. For it is by believing in your heart that you are made right with God, and it is by confessing with your mouth that you are saved." (Rom. 10:9-10, NLT)

It's that simple! We are not saved by our good deeds. Our good deeds could never earn us a place in His Kingdom. For if that was true, Christ died in vain. We are saved by His grace. It is a free gift that we cannot earn. All we have to do to receive is to renounce living for ourselves and commit our life to Him as Lord, which means Supreme Master. "He died for all, that those who live should live no longer for themselves, but for Him who died for them and rose again." (2 Cor. 5:15)

So if you believe Christ died for you, and you are willing to give Him your life and no longer live for yourself; then we can pray this prayer together and you will become a child of God:

God in Heaven, I acknowledge that I am a sinner and have fallen short of Your righteous standard. I deserve to be judged for eternity for my sin. Thank You for not leaving me in this state, for I believe you sent Jesus Christ, Your only begotten

Son, who was born of the Virgin Mary, to die for me and carry my judgment on the Cross. I believe He was raised again on the third day and is now seated at Your right hand as my Lord and Savior. So on this day of _____, 20__, I give my life entirely to the Lordship of Jesus.

Jesus, I confess you as my Lord and Savior. Come into my life through Your Spirit and change me into a child of God. I renounce the things of darkness which I once held on to, and from this day forward I will no longer live for myself, but for You who gave Yourself for me that I may live forever.

Thank You Lord; my life is now completely in Your hands and heart, and according to Your Word I shall never be ashamed.

Now, you are saved; you are a child of God. All heaven is rejoicing with you at this very moment! Welcome to the family!

HOW TO BE FILLED WITH THE HOLY SPIRIT

Receiving the fullness of the Holy Spirit is as easy as receiving Jesus as your Lord and Savior. Some struggle, become discouraged, and can't receive most often due to the neglect of receiving basic scriptural instructions before asking. I've learned it is always best to show seekers what God says before praying, as this develops their faith to receive. So before I lead you in a prayer to receive, allow me first to instruct.

First and foremost, you must have already received Jesus Christ as your personal Lord and Savior (see John 14:17).

There can be no pattern of disobedience in your life. We are told that God gives His Spirit "to those who obey Him" (Acts 5:32). I've learned from experience this especially includes the area of unforgiveness. In our meetings I've seen many times hundreds receive the Holy Spirit and immediately speak in other tongues, yet a dozen or two of the hundreds stand and look bewildered. In almost every case in going to those few dozen I would find the Lord leading me to deal with harbored offense. Once the seekers forgave they immediately received and spoke in tongues. So before we go any further let's pray together.

Father, I ask that you would search me and show me if there is any disobedience in my heart. Please show me if there is any person I have withheld forgiveness from. I purpose to obey and forgive no matter what You reveal to me. I ask this in the name of Jesus and thank You so very much.

To receive the Holy Spirit all you have to do is ask! Jesus simply says, "If a son asks for bread from any father among you, will he give him a stone? Or if he asks for a fish, will he give him a serpent instead of a fish? Or if he asks for an egg, will he offer him a scorpion? If you then, being evil, know how to give good gifts to your children, how much more will your heavenly Father give the Holy Spirit to those who ask Him!" (Luke 11:11-13). He is simply saying that if our children ask us for something which is our will to give them, we won't give them something evil or different. In the same way, if you ask the Father for His Spirit, He won't give you an evil spirit. All you have to do is ask the Father in Jesus' name, and you will receive His Holy Spirit.

You must ask in faith. The New Testament tell us it is impossible to receive from God without faith. James 1:6-7 states: "But let him ask in faith, with no doubting, for he who doubts is like a wave of the sea driven and tossed by the wind. For let not that man suppose that he will receive anything from the Lord. So ask yourself at this moment, "When will I receive? Will it be when I speak in other tongues, or will it be the moment I ask?" Your answer should be - the moment you ask! For in the Kingdom, we believe then receive. Those who do not have faith say, "Show me and I will believe" but Jesus says, "I say to you, whatever things you ask when you pray, believe that you receive them, and you will have them" (Mark 11:24). Notice you believe first, and then you will have what you've asked for.

Acts 2:4 says, "And they were all filled with the Holy Spirit and began to speak with other tongues, as the Spirit gave them utterance." Notice they spoke with tongues; it was not the Holy Spirit who spoke in tongues. They had to do it, as the Spirit gave them the words. So there is a yielding! I can be in a swift moving river, but if I don't pick up my feet and yield to the river, I won't flow with it. So there are three areas we must yield: First, our lips. If I don't move my lips, words, whether in English or in a Foreign language, a heavenly tongue cannot come forth. Second, our tongue. If I don't move my tongue, I cannot speak. Third, our vocal chords. If I don't yield my vocal cords to my lungs, then I cannot speak.

You may at this point think I'm being sarcastic, but I'm not. After years of seeing people struggle, I've learned many subconsciously think the Holy Spirit is going to grab ahold of their lips, tongues, and vocal cords and make them speak. No, we speak, or yield, as He gives the utterance.

Jesus says, "'He who believes in Me, as the Scripture has said, out of his heart will flow rivers of living water.' But this He spoke concerning the Spirit, whom those believing in Him would receive; for the Holy Spirit was not yet given, because Jesus was not yet glorified" (John 7:38-39). When you ask for the Holy Spirit, you may have a syllable bubbling up, or rolling around in your head. If you will speak it in faith, it will be as if you open a dam, and the language will come forth. I like to see it as a spool of thread in your gut and the tip, or beginning of the thread, is glimpsed at your tongue, but as you begin to pull (speak), out comes the rest of the thread. Some think they are going to have the entire language in their mind then they will speak. No, we are to speak in faith.

I remember when my wife prayed to receive the Holy Spirit she didn't speak in tongues for a time, then she and a few friends were praying a few weeks later and she began to speak in tongues. She then said, "I had that syllable running through my head the past few weeks while praying, but didn't yield to it till tonight." I believe this is the case for so many - they ask, receive, but don't yield.

Scripture states, "The spirits of the prophets [spokespersons] are subject to the prophets" (1 Cor 14:32). This simply tells us that we are the ones who speak, and that the Holy Spirit will not force Himself on us. I recall the day after I was filled with the Holy Spirit I didn't know how to speak again. I went to another brother at the gym and asked, "How can I do it again?" He said, "John, you just do it!" I went out for a run and began to speak in tongues again while running. I was overcome with joy. We must remember the Holy Spirit is always ready to go; we are the ones who must yield. It is like a water fountain. The water is always there; all you have to do is turn the knob and out comes the water. So pray in tongues frequently!

Now that you have received basic instructions from the Scripture, if you believe you will receive we can pray together. One last thing: you cannot speak English and Spanish at the same time. Even so you can't speak in English and tongues at the same time. So remember, just believe and yield! Let's pray:

Father, in the name of Jesus, I come to you as Your child. You said if I asked You for the Holy Spirit You would give Him to me. With joy I now ask in faith; please baptize and fill me at this very moment with Your Holy Spirit. I receive all You have for me including the ability to speak in tongues. So now in faith I will speak in new tongues! Amen!

Notes

MISSION THREE

1. E. M. Bounds, "The Wrath of God," *Prayer and Revival*, edited by Darrel D. King (Grand Rapids, MI: Baker Publishing Group, 1993), 41.

2. Bounds, "Christ's Lessons in Fear," *Prayer and Revival*, 33-34.

3. A. W. Tozer, "God Incomprehensible," *The Knowledge of the Holy* (San Francisco: HarperSanFrancisco, 1978), 6.

4. Ibid., 10.

MISSION FIVE

5. Charles G. Finney, "Holiness for Christians in the Present Life," 1843, in *Principles of Holiness* (Minneapolis, MN: Bethany House Publishers, 1984), 20.

6. Ibid., 36

7. Charles G. Finney, "Preaching as a Missionary," *Charles Finney: An Autobiography* (Grand Rapids, MI: Fleming H. Revell, 1975), 67.

8. Finney, "Revival at Rome," *Charles Finney: An Autobiography*, 166.

MISSION NINE

9. The American Heritage Dictionary of the English Language, Fourth Edition (Boston: Houghton Mifflin Company, 2000), s.v. "insidious."

MISSION ELEVEN

10. Leonard Ravenhill, *America Is Too Young to Die* (Minneapolis, MN: Bethany House, 1979), 71.

11. Ibid., 72.

Driven by Eternity *(Release date March 2006)*

Making Your Life Count Today & Forever

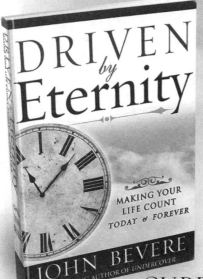

We were made for eternity. This life on earth is but a vapor. Yet too many live as though there is nothing on the other side. Scriptural laws and principles may be applied to achieve success on earth, but are we prepared for eternity? Have we failed to remember we will all stand before the Great Judge of Heaven and Earth?

Scripture tells us there will be various degrees of rewards for believers ranging from those who watch as all they accomplished is devoured in judgment to those who are awarded the privilege to reign with Christ. These judgments will determine how we spend our span of eternity.

Included in this book is a riveting allegory. It takes place in a world similar to our own, yet different. Lord Jalyn is the ruler of the Kingdom of Affabel. You will journey with six of his subjects through their lives, witness their judgment, and see how and where they will spend the rest of their lives. The teaching of this book revolves around the lessons learned from their lives.

CURRICULUM RELEASE JUNE 2006

Fight Like a Girl *(Release date April 2006)*

The Power of Being a Woman

Why is it that women often don't like women? What could possibly cause a large portion of us to reject our own gender? More often than not we lack an appreciation for women. We associate men with strength and women with weakness. We therefore attempt life in roles as men, only to find ourselves conflicted. But God is awakening and empowering His daughters to realize who they truly are, as well as their unique and significant contributions. In order to find our way we must first turn off the ever-present negative noise surrounding us as women. What does this static say?

"Women are a problem"

Have you heard it? Notice I did not say women can cause problems, for surely they can, but that women are a problem. This ancient lie has worked against us since the garden, but I have discovered for every lie there is an overriding truth.

"Women are not a problem, they are an answer"

As the curtains of time draw to a close, women will be restored to fight the battles they are called to wage and to confront the enemy who has robbed them for so long. It is time we stop hiding in the guise of male and begin to fight like a girl!

Please contact us today to receive your free copy of Messenger International's *Messenger* newsletter and our 32 page color catalog of ministry resources!

The vision of MI is to strengthen believers, awaken the lost and captive in the church and proclaim the knowledge of His glory to the nations. John and Lisa are reaching millions of people each year through television and by ministering at churches, bible schools and conferences around the world. We long to see God's Word in the hands of leaders and hungry believers in every part of the earth.

MESSENGER INTERNATIONAL

www.messengerintl.org

UNITED STATES
PO Box 888
Palmer Lake, CO 80133-0888
800-648-1477 (US & Canada)
Tel: 719-487-3000
Fax: 719-487-3300
E-mail: mail@messengerintl.org

EUROPE
PO Box 622
Newport, NP19 8ZJ
UNITED KINGDOM
Tel: 44 (0) 870-745-5790
Fax: 44 (0) 870-745-5791
E-mail: europe@messengerintl.org

AUSTRALIA
PO Box 6200
Dural, D.C. NSW 2158
Australia
In AUS 1-300-650-577
Tel: +61 2 8850 1725
Fax +61 2 8850 1735
Email: australia@messengerintl.org

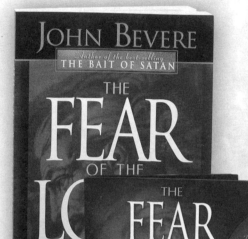

4 CD SERIES

The Fear of the Lord
Discover the Key to Intimately Knowing God

More than ever, there's something missing in our churches, our prayers and in our personal lives. It's what builds intimacy in our relationship with God. It's what makes our lives real and pure. It's what transforms us into truly Spirit-led children of God. It is the fear of the Lord.

Fit For the Kingdom - 8 CDs
The Truth About Eternal Greatness... will you receive full, partial or no reward.

You were created for eternity. This life is but a vapor. Yet too many live as though nothing is on the other side. Could it be we have forgotten we will all stand before the Great Judge? Then there will be various degrees of awards ranging from those whose accomplishments go up in smoke to those who are awarded the privilege of reigning with Christ. Your choices now will determine how you spend eternity

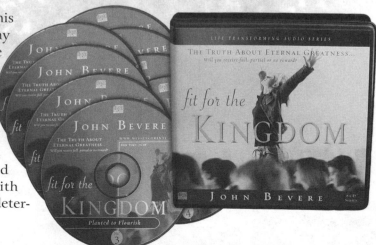

Based on her National Best-selling book with over 100,000 copies sold, Lisa Bevere now answers the requests of thousands of women, youth and Bible study groups with the release of this unique and comprehensive curriculum! With Lisa's personally written workbook, *Kissed the Girls and Made Them Cry* is an answer to the heart-cry of women of all ages everywhere!

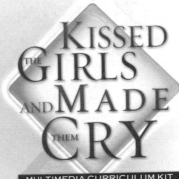

KISSED THE GIRLS AND MADE THEM CRY

MULTIMEDIA CURRICULUM KIT

It's perfect for...

WOMEN'S & YOUTH GROUPS

MOTHERS & DAUGHTERS

INDIVIDUALS

INCLUDES:
- 4 DVDs
- 5 VHS Tapes including the 4 lessons, bonus Q&A, testimonies, and personal messages from Lisa
- 4 corresponding CDs
- 1 Best-selling <u>Kissed the Girls and Made them Cry</u> book
- 1 Interactive Workbook
- 1 <u>Desperation Band</u> music CD

...AND MORE

UNDER COVER

MULTIMEDIA CURRICULUM KIT

The Promise of Protection Under His Authority

LET'S FACE IT, authority is not a popular word, yet by rejecting it, we lose the great protection, provision, promotion and freedom authority provides. If you embrace these principles, living under authority will liberate you rather then restrain you.

INCLUDES:
- 12 lessons on 5 VHS Tapes
- 2 DVD's
- 6 CD's
- 1 Best-selling <u>Under Cover</u> book
- 1 Leader's guide
- 1 Workbook

#1 Seller for Churches and Bible Studies